WHAT NEXT AT WORK?

Alastair Evans was born in London and educated at Emanuel School, Wandsworth. He has an MA in Industrial Relations from the University of Warwick, a Diploma in Personnel Management from Middlesex Polytechnic and is a Member of the IPM.

The author spent a number of years working in the personnel department of a large company in the brewing industry where he was involved in all aspects of company personnel work. This was followed by a period of study and research at Warwick and City Universities before taking up a post in the Research and Planning division of the Department of Employment. The author currently holds the post of Manager – Organization and Manpower Planning at the IPM and is also a visiting Lecturer in Industrial Sociology at the Polytechnic of North London.

Alastair Evans has published a number of articles on personnel management and industrial relations and is currently working on further publications for IPM concerned with recruitment, manpower information and the role of the personnel manager in technical change.

What next at work?

A NEW CHALLENGE FOR MANAGERS

Alastair Evans

Institute of Personnel Management

© *Institute of Personnel Management 1979*
First Published 1979

Printed in Great Britain by Lonsdale Universal Printing Ltd.

ISBN 0 85292 256 6

Contents

Acknowledgements   *vi*
Foreword   *vii*
Introduction   I

PART ONE : THE LEGACY OF THE PAST
  I Economic change and the industrial relations system   7
  2 Social change and attitudes to work   21

PART TWO : TODAY AND TOMORROW
  3 The changing labour market   27
  4 Changing technology   46
  5 Changing employment law   51
  6 Changing educational output   58
  The argument so far   64

PART THREE : SOME MAJOR ISSUES FOR ORGANIZAT-
   IONS
  7 Unemployment and worksharing   69
  8 Technological change and organizations   88
  9 The impact of the legal framework   103
10 Education and working life   109

PART FOUR : SUMMARY AND IMPLICATIONS
11 Summary   121
12 Some implications for personnel specialists   126
Appendix   139
References   143
Sources for data   155
Bibliography   157
Index   163

Acknowledgements

The author wishes to acknowledge the great debt owed to Chris Hayes and the IPM's National Committee for Organization and Manpower Planning for their inspiration, encouragement and comment throughout the duration of the project which led to this publication. Acknowledgement also goes to those from industry, government and academia who attended a seminar to discuss this publication and to the many members of IPM Branches around the country who passed their comment on what is contained within. Their suggestions were much appreciated, but the responsibility for remaining errors are those of the author alone.

Foreword

This is a book for all managers who find the change in our industrial climate since the oil crisis perplexing. It should be particularly helpful to personnel managers as members of an organization's management team. In the opinion of the IPM's National Committee on Organization and Manpower Planning the book is badly needed, since current changes are creating a fundamentally new situation in which traditional actions lead to unexpected and often undesirable results. We believe that the key to understanding what is happening is to grasp the combined impact of various changes in the environment of enterprises and especially the combination of arrested economic growth and high unemployment. The strength of this book rests therefore neither on original research nor on an exposition of common sense; nor do we believe in quick fashionable remedies. Alastair Evans has succeeded in bringing together in one place all the major issues and he shows that in turn any successful response by an enterprise must meet all the issues by integrating the traditionally fragmented reactions of an organization. Certainly within the personnel function, manpower planning, employee relations, industrial relations and employee development must act jointly.

The National Committee has been able to test this line of reasoning through two seminars – one with branch officers and one with senior people of great experience – and we were glad to see our views wholeheartedly confirmed. The author has managed to present the facts, issues and options in a concise and highly readable manner. It is now up to readers to decide how they should act. Individual managers cannot change our industrial society but unless each of us does his or her bit in the new situation we must not be surprised if our competitive standing as a country continues to deteriorate. We hope this book will be one such contribution.

Chris Hayes
Vice-President
Organization and Manpower Planning

Introduction

For many managers the 1970s proved to be a tortuous period, one in which the growth of employment and other legislation, low rates of economic growth, industrial relations difficulties and inflation seemed to be combining to make the task of management more frustrating and less rewarding. Faced with such changes, many managers began to feel that they could not see 'the wood from the trees'.

The purpose of this book is to try and separate 'the wood from the trees', to highlight a number of key changes which are making the management of people at work substantially different from even a decade ago and to suggest what the implications of these changes might be for managers.

Change in the environment surrounding organizations is the most appropriate starting point for understanding the source of pressure for change within organizations. Organizations do not exist in a vacuum: the economic climate, social attitudes, technology, legal and political forces are constraints which all impinge on their success or failure. The challenge for organizations is to adapt policies and practices to meet the changing environment.[1] Recent history is littered with examples of organizations which have failed to adapt old products to new market conditions or firms which have failed to adopt more efficient technology, with low productivity and lack of price competitiveness being the almost inevitable result. For organizations which fail to adapt to these key changes in their environment, the result can be debilitation and even demise. Less obvious, but nevertheless important, is the impact on organizational effectiveness of changes in the environment relating to people in organizations. It is on this that we shall be concentrating our attention in highlighting key changes facing managers.

The major changes which will be considered may be outlined as follows and under each heading some questions will be raised which the book aims to consider. *Economic change* is affecting the nature of the environment in which our organizations

[1] All references are listed on page 143

operate. For most of the post-war period the economic climate was one of relatively high rates of economic growth, an expanding demand for goods and services and low levels of unemployment. But recent experience and future projections indicate slower rates of economic growth than in this earlier period, rising unemployment and further competition from the newly-industrializing nations, leading to a further decline in our traditional manufacturing industries. Most organizations will not be able to expand as in the past, with all the implications this has for career prospects, job security and redundancy. How are organizations to cope with this and how also will trade unions react to rising unemployment? Does this mean increased resistance to redundancy or pressures to reduce working time to spread the available work amongst those who are unemployed?

Demographic (ie population) *changes* are also occurring which are causing a substantial increase in the size of the workforce at a time when doubts are being expressed about the expansion of job opportunities. Could such changes add to the pressure by trade unions for measures aimed at reducing unemployment?

Marked *social changes* took place during the affluent post-war decades. People's expectations rose and now people continue to expect job security and rises in living standards, while at the same time organizations, faced with a low growth in demand for their goods and services, will find it increasingly difficult to meet these aspirations. What alternatives are open to organizations in this situation?

Technical change and its accompanying problems of obsolescence of old skills and the need to retrain in new ones is nothing new but recent developments in microelectronics suggest that most organizations are likely to implement substantial technical changes which will have implications from senior manager to shop floor. What are these changes and their implications for organizations, particularly their impact on managers, trade unions and employees as a whole?

The growth of *legal intervention* in the traditionally 'voluntarist' system of industrial relations in Britain has led to a reduction in dismissals and an increase in the cost of declaring redundancies. With employees becoming 'fixed' rather than 'variable' assets to organizations, what should management be doing to cope with this change?

Educational change presents organizations with a number of contradictory forces. A number of employers feel that many

2

school leavers lack certain basic skills, while statistics show that the nation as a whole is producing more qualified people, both at school and higher education levels. While any remedy to the first of these contentions is largely the responsibility of the educational authorities, the second presents a new challenge to organizations. As educational attainments rise, so also do aspirations and expectations: for more intrinsically interesting work, for an opportunity to participate in decision-making, for promotion and advancement. Yet many young people entering work for the first time, both qualified school leaver and graduate, do so at much lower levels in organizations than hitherto and face poorer prospects of promotion within an economic environment of low growth. How can organizations attract and retain the calibre of new employee which they require at a time when meeting the demands of qualified staff is becoming increasingly problematic?

In addition to these new developments, many of the key issues which managers also face are legacies of the post-war era of growth and it is to this area that we turn our attention in part I. As suggested above, a number of current changes which are significantly different from the past may be identified and these are considered in part II. Part III goes on to enlarge on the organizational impact of the major aspects of change previously identified. Part IV summarizes the arguments and discusses the role of the personnel specialist in assisting organizations to manage with change.

Part one

THE LEGACY OF THE PAST

1

Economic change and the industrial relations system

Any examination of the problems facing those concerned with managing change now or in the near future must begin by looking at the problems inherited from the past. Many past problems may of course be 'water under the bridge', but many other problems persist and many aspects of the environment facing managers have their origins here. Moreover, many of our present policies owe their existence to the past and ought to be re-examined in that light. Hence the need to make a start here.

Having said in the introduction that many of the issues confronting managers have their origins outside the organizations within which they work, a key starting point is to examine the UK economy. It is here that many of the issues, both past and present, facing organizations may be found. The next few pages will highlight the recent history of the UK economy, particularly those aspects of the economic environment which have had a direct influence on issues and problems faced by those concerned with the management of people at work.

An appropriate place to start a discussion of these relevant economic changes follows the watershed created by the last war. Looking back today over the last two or three decades, the period has been characterized by a substantial growth in the living standards of the nation. Taking some measures of this, during this period house ownership increased from less than one third to over one half of all houses, average earnings increased almost sevenfold, while consumer prices by just over fourfold, hours of work became shorter, paid holidays longer, and the ownership of cars, TVs and labour-saving or luxury household goods

7

multiplied many times.[2] Yet despite this, the best part of the last two decades has been occupied by a debate on the causes of Britain's economic and industrial decline. Abroad, such epithets as 'The Sick Man of Europe' or 'The British Disease' have been coined to describe this condition. It is important therefore to look more closely at this latter phenomenon and the explanations which have been offered.

The arrival of full employment

A useful starting point is the post-war commitment to a policy of full employment. The pre-war years had been characterized by 'trade cycles' involving boom years of relatively high levels of employment interspersed with depressions when unemployment rose sharply. The average annual level of unemployment between 1921–1939 was 14 per cent, although rates in excess of 50 per cent were recorded in regions such as North-East England, Central Scotland, South Wales and Northern Ireland. A White Paper, *Full Employment In A Free Society* produced by Lord Beveridge in 1944 paved the way for the adoption of a welfare state and full employment. It marked also a fundamental change in the approach of government to the management of the economy. The economic policies of government before the war had been based upon an economic theory which held that unemployment resulted because wages had been forced to levels which the employer could not afford given the prevailing market price for his products. To reduce unemployment it was necessary to reduce wage levels. A very different view was taken by J M (later Lord) Keynes whose new theories strongly influenced the 1944 White Paper. His view was that unemployment was the result of deficient demand in the economy and advocated a much more active role for the government requiring increased public expenditure to stimulate demand when unemployment began to rise. Lord Beveridge's White Paper aimed to keep unemployment to a maximum of three per cent. In the event, Keynesian policies exceeded Beveridge's expectations, the rate of unemployment never rose above three per cent until after 1970 and from the late 1940s to the mid 1960s unemployment generally remained at between one and a half and two per cent.

The onset of economic difficulty

The post-war decade was characterized by a boom in world trade from which Britain benefited. From about the mid 1950s, however, the trading environment began to change. Post-war reconstruction in West Germany, the remainder of Western Europe and Japan considerably increased the competition in the market place and put further pressure on British manufacturers to modernize production and to control costs, especially wage costs. In fact wages and prices in the post-war British economy had shown a persistent tendency to inflate and this, aligned with a slow growth in productivity, was forcing up employers' unit costs. Associated with this were periodic and recurrent balance of payments crises in which the economy tended to suck in imports, while inflation reduced the price-competitiveness of our exports. Governments were therefore forced periodically to damp down demand in the economy in what have been referred to as 'stop–go' policies.

Although it is impossible to be precise about a date, the late 1950s and early 1960s saw the emergence of a debate on the underlying problems of the UK economy which became particularly acute during the financial crisis of 1961. Of particular concern was why Britain should be at or near the bottom of the international table of economic growth. Numerous factors were suggested : poor quality of management, low levels of investment, lack of expertise in the Civil Service, the loss of the ready markets of the British Empire and shortcomings in the educational system. A persistent line of criticism to emerge was related to the British industrial relations system. What kind of effect did strikes have on industrial output and competitiveness in export markets ; union wage demands on inflation ; and the restrictive practices of trade unions on productivity, economic growth and industrial change?

The pressures of full employment

The analysis of the problem goes something like this and highlights the significance of the post-war commitment to full employment. The arrival of full employment brought about a fundamental change in the labour market. Under the pre-war conditions of unemployment, labour was plentiful. With full employment labour markets became 'tight', there ceased to be

9

queues of unemployed at the labour exchange, labour was in short supply and recruitment became a difficult problem. Mary Niven has provided a vivid description of this change from the perspective of the personnel officer at this time:

It became necessary to attract staff to a firm, instead of picking and choosing, and blandishments were used. Advertisements crept into the press offering 'excellent welfare, canteen and social facilities' with barely a mention of work. Wages and salaries for the scarcest categories of staff soon began to soar as competition for them grew.[3]

The arrival of full employment created competition between employers who tried to outbid each other to attract labour to meet the rising demands for their goods created by the post-war industrial boom. Although many employers were members of their industry's employers' federation, wage rates and fringe benefits in many local labour markets exceeded those fixed by national agreements.

Full employment brought about a further very significant change, the transformation of power relations between management and unions at the workplace. The nature of these changes are described by Allan Flanders:

On the one hand, management finds the negative sanctions which it had customarily employed to uphold its authority are weakened: the strength of the ultimate penalty of the sack has diminished to the extent that workers can easily find alternative employment . . . On the other hand, shop stewards have less fear of victimization and workgroups can assert their collective will on a management which is decidedly more vulnerable to pressure when the order books are full.[4]

The shift from unemployment to full employment swung the pendulum of bargaining power from the employer towards the union. Not only towards union leaders and unions as national organizations, but also towards work groups in factories at the local level where production pressures and recruitment difficulties really lay. It was the growth of this system of industrial relations which the Donovan Commission later referred to as the conflict between the formal national and informal local system of bargaining and diagnosed to be at the root of British industrial relations problems.[5]

The significance of the development of this system for post-war economic performance goes deeper than has already been suggested. The origins of an inflationary spiral, with employers bidding up wage levels against each other and work groups in the plant using their new-found bargaining power to secure extra payments, have been outlined. But certain other problems arose out of plant bargaining under full employment which further accentuated these problems.

First, there was the problem of 'wage drift'. Systems of 'payment by results' had become more widespread and by 1951 affected 28 per cent of male manual workers as against 18 per cent in 1938.[6] 'Wage drift', which refers to the tendency for wages in the workplace to rise above nationally-agreed rates, has been described as 'one of the most important and characteristic phenomena of post-war inflation'.[7] The role of piecework payments in wage drift is a topic worthy of lengthier discussion than is possible here. Suffice to say that severe problems surrounded the relationship between effort and reward and over a period of time, as a result of technical change and work group manipulation, the bonus payment became more generous than had originally been intended.[8] Add to this the problem of maintaining traditional intra-plant differentials, for example between craft and production workers, and it was not difficult to understand why many plants became arenas of almost continuous competitive bargaining between fragmented work groups, adding to the inflationary spiral by increasing wage rates with little or no relationship to effort or output.

One further very important problem emerged in the post-war industrial relations system. It has already been suggested that pay systems became so chaotic that management lost control over the effort–reward relationship. If people are effectively paid more to produce less, manpower is underutilized, unit labour costs rise and productivity falls. Other instances of a more sensational variety of the underemployment of labour hit the newspaper headlines in the late 1950s and are generally grouped together as 'restrictive practices'. A restrictive practice, which is essentially a restriction on the employer's recruitment or deployment of labour imposed unilaterally by a union or work group, was not of course a new phenomenon to emerge in the post-war period.

The Webbs' analysis of nineteenth century trade unionism noted that 'demarcation' between crafts was as old as trade unionism itself and the control of entry of apprentices into a craft predated it.[9] Nevertheless changes in the post-war economy seemed to accentuate the problem. Traditional demarcation lines between crafts were being rendered obsolete as a result of changed technology. The same applied to the maintenance of traditional manning levels of machines. Craftsmen's mates continued to be employed as the craftsmen's traditional status symbol rather than out of the need—indeed evidence suggested that many mates actually worked for less than half the time each day.[10] Finally, overtime, once introduced to meet a specific production need, became a guaranteed element in the pay packet and further served to attract labour to the firm. In conclusion, the tight labour market created by full employment may have made employers reluctant to act to cut back on underemployment practices for fear of losing labour, especially scarce skills which could not easily be replaced, and of alienating a workforce with newly-found bargaining powers.

The diagnosis of the problems of the British economy as it emerged amongst official policy-makers in the early 1960s may be summarized as follows. Under the tight labour market conditions of full employment, the role of free collective bargaining at plant level, coupled with the widespread adoption of poorly-controlled piecework payment systems, was essentially inflationary. Moreover, there was extensive underutilization of manpower, associated both with the restrictive practices of trade unions and the failure of many employers to adequately control payment systems and shake our excess labour. Problems of labour shortages were further compounded by a marked shortage of skilled craftsmen. In addition, a further problem was felt to be emerging, the growth of unofficial strikes. Although in the country as a whole neither total days lost nor total number of disputes showed any constant tendency to rise in the 1950s or early 1960s, a decline in the strike proneness in the mining industry was being compensated by a growth of strikes in other industries.

The emergence of government intervention

Up to the late 1950s, the prevailing attitude was that these problems were industry's and it was industry's problem to find a solution. In the early 1960s, however, the concept of planning re-emerged as a major theme of government policy. A recent analysis edited by Blackaby has suggested that this was

12

stimulated by the growing practice of making international comparisons which highlighted Britain's comparatively poor record of investment and productivity and the need for longer term planning of public expenditure.[11] It was out of this new policy that the National Economic Development Council (NEDC) was established in 1961 and it was the NEDC which was soon to emphasize the importance of manpower and training policies in achieving faster growth.[12]

Before looking at the emerging role of government in manpower matters in the 1960s, the change was sufficiently significant to warrant a closer examination of the role of law in relation to employment prior to this time. A prominent labour lawyer in Britain, Professor Otto Kahn Freund, once wrote:

> There is, perhaps, no major country in the world in which the law has played a less significant role in the shaping of (industrial) relations than in Great Britain.[13]

Such a system has been widely referred to as 'voluntarism', implying a preference for voluntary agreement between employers and trade unions within a framework of free collective bargaining unfettered by interference from government or the courts. This is not to imply that the state had no place in the regulation of relationships at work. Legislation dating from the nineteenth and early twentieth century laid down health and safety regulations under various Factories Acts from 1833, payment of wages was controlled by Truck Acts dating from 1831, state arbitration in disputes dated from an 1896 Act and minimum wage legislation dates from the Trade Boards Act of 1909. But the role of government was one of minimum intervention and the application of very minimum standards of wages or conditions. The system of voluntarism suited trade unions and employers. British trade unions in the twentieth century had dropped the legislative platform that had been central to their objectives of the nineteenth century. Experience of nineteenth century judgements culminating in the famous 'Taff Vale' case in 1901, which resulted in a union paying substantial damages to the employer, suggested that the law had little to give them and a preference grew for achieving improvements in pay and conditions through free collective bargaining. Employers also, generally opposed to outside state interference, grew to support this concept, holding the view that the parties to a bargain (management and unions) were better able to control their affairs to mutual advantage than lawyers or government officials who did not understand the problems of industry.

A number of changes in the post-war economy drew the government further into an interventionist role. The adoption of Keynesian economic strategies of demand management by implication meant a more active role in industry. The establishment of the welfare state and the public ownership of many industries, in addition to the large and growing number of industrial and non-industrial civil servants, meant that the government had become the nation's biggest employer, employing about a quarter of the total working population. These changes, in addition to direct attempts to control the rate of inflationary wage increases through incomes policies (which dated from 1948) and an increase in arbitration in industrial disputes, were such that by the late 1950s the role of government in industrial relations had already begun to increase.

The growth of legislation

Given the manpower utilization and industrial relations problems being identified in the 1950s, it was therefore no great surprise that the early 1960s would witness the decline of voluntarism, although it occurred as a response to growing economic difficulties rather than as the result of union or employer pressure to legislate. Although some attempts to promote social justice may have underlain the legislation, much of it was concerned with the need to make more efficient use of manpower and encourage industrial peace by removing some of the causes of conflict. The legislative and other government policies adopted during the 1960s and 1970s varied in emphasis according to the diagnosis of the problem by policy makers. On the one hand there was concern with the manifestations of the disorder within the industrial relations system, the growth of unofficial (unsanctioned by the union) and unconstitutional (in disregard of disputes procedures) strikes and their harmful effects on the economy. On the other hand, there was concern with the underutilization of manpower and its depressive effect on productivity which were seen as the result of a failure of existing industrial relations institutions, particularly fragmented bargaining, to achieve change. The Contracts of Employment Act (1963) fell into the latter category. Rather than promote labour mobility with the objective of reducing underemployment of labour, it provided

14

employees with greater job security by laying down minimum periods of notice which extended with length of service. The Act also required the issue to employees of a written memorandum of the terms and conditions of employment, which might, if expressly stated, include the obligation to abide by existing collective agreements between company and union. Since there was also likely to be a disputes procedure, observance of this became a term of the contract. In his review of the development of government industrial relations policies, Moran has concluded that:

> (The) carrot of security was accompanied by a stick: workers who engaged in unconstitutional industrial action would be deemed to have broken their continuity of employment and to have thus forfeited their rights under the Act.[14]

While the Contracts of Employment Act was aimed at enhancing individual rights and the problem of unconstitutional strikes, the Redundancy Payments Act of 1965 focussed attention again on manpower problems. According to a Department of Employment survey in 1969 the Act

> . . . was designed to fulfil two main purposes, one economic and the other social. On the economic side, it was intended to facilitate a more effective utilization of manpower by reducing the economic consequences of redundancy to those affected. On the social side, it was recognized that the individual has some rights in his job, in the same way as the employer holds rights in his property, and that these accumulate in value over time. The purpose of the Act in this sphere was to provide some notional compensation for the losses individuals may suffer as a consequence of redundancy.[15]

The Act aimed at providing compensation, which increased with age and length of service, in order to reduce employee and union resistance to reductions in manning necessitated by technical or organizational change. In the tight labour market conditions still prevailing in the early 1960s and with the persistent shortage of skilled manpower hampering growth, it was hoped that a 'shake out' of underutilized manpower would result. In the years following the Act, Department of Employment figures indicated that the number of paid redundancies rose from over 26,000 in 1966 to over 108,000 in 1971.[16] Allowing for employees with less than two years service who were excluded from the Act, estimates suggest that the figure for all redundancies could have risen from less than half a million in the early 1960s to between three-quarters and one million by 1970.[17] Although the Act may have made a contribution to the problem of manpower underutilization, overall it probably tended to shake out unskilled workers rather than the skilled who were in short supply.

The increased government involvement in training stemming from the Industrial Training Act of 1964 and the establishment of 27 Industrial Training Boards between 1964 and 1969 also resulted from the manpower utilization and manpower shortage critique of the economy which had emerged in the post-war period. According to Hughes, prior to 1963 the government's role in training had been purely social.[18] Government Training Centres had been set up in the 1920s to provide skilled training for those disabled in World War I and continued through to the 1950s to concentrate on the needs of ex-regular servicemen and the disabled, with little or no emphasis on eliminating the skill shortages which were emerging. From 1963, Hughes argues:

> ... the emphasis of the programme was changed from social to economic. The objective was no longer simply to enhance the employability of particular groups without regard to general labour market conditions but to tackle labour market bottlenecks by directing training at skill shortage occupations.[19]

A review of the Act in *Training for the Future*[20] indicated that it had made a substantial contribution to the growth of systematic training, particularly in the field of apprenticeship training. But the review was critical of the difficulties inherent in a structure based on an industry to meet the training needs of occupations crossing industrial boundaries. It was also critical of the problems of dealing with regional or local labour market needs where particular skill shortages existed or where unemployment was growing as a result of industrial decline. This implied the need for a more co-ordinated manpower policy involving national training and employment needs, an approach which we shall see later emerging in the mid 1970s.

Incomes policies and productivity bargaining

One aspect of government policies in the 1960s aimed at the promotion of manpower objectives was incomes policy. Although incomes policies had been tried in Britain between 1948 and 1950 and the government had attempted to impose voluntary restraint, particularly on the public sector in the middle to late 1950s, modern incomes policy really stems from the 'pay pause' of 1961–62. This short lived policy was followed by a more extensive period of incomes policy administered through the Prices and Incomes Board between 1965 and 1969. The argument for an incomes policy went something like this. There was growing evidence to support the view that annual wage increases which exceeded annual growth in productivity were inflationary. Employers' cost increases could be reflected in price increases, giving rise to further wage demands to compensate and a price/wage inflationary spiral. In addition, this process adversely affected the price competitiveness of UK exports with an accompanying adverse effect on the balance of payments. While it is beyond the scope of this discussion to go into the details of incomes policies pursued in the 1960s, some salient points need to be raised in the light of our general discussion.[21] First, a 'norm' for wage increases was established which was intended to reflect annual growth in productivity (in the region of two and a half per cent). Wage settlements in excess of this figure would only be justified on grounds of additional productivity over and above the norm. This latter qualification was aimed at placing more emphasis on improved manpower utilization and productivity in wage bargaining. Indeed further stimulus was given to this by the publication in 1964 of an influential and widely-read book by Allan Flanders on the productivity bargain struck at the Esso Refinery in Fawley.[22] This study suggested that not only could productivity bargaining secure substantial alterations in work practices to reduce overmanning, unnecessary overtime and demarcation, but could substantially improve industrial relations within the firm through the formalization of plant bargaining. Bargaining would no longer be 'ad hoc' and conducted with fragmented work groups, but would involve local management and the local representatives of all unions concerned (full-time officers and shop stewards) in concluding an all-embracing plant bargain.

The report of the Donovan Commission on Trade Unions and Employers Associated published in 1968 echoed the role of plant bargaining advocated by Flanders in achieving manpower and industrial relations objectives. But the optimism generated by these proposals was to be short lived. The incidence of unofficial strikes, and indeed major national official strikes, grew in the late

1960s. Four thousand productivity bargains covering over seven million workers had been concluded. Many of them were not of the far-reaching nature envisaged by Flanders, serving more as a way round incomes policy rather than adding to productivity or assisting the problems of manpower utilization. Moreover, given the role of comparability in pay claims, the high settlements agreed in genuine productivity bargains became the 'going rate' for other claims not based on productivity. This generally raised aspirations for future settlements to the extent that it has been suggested that it helped to generate a wage explosion in 1969.[23] The passing of the Industrial Relations Act in 1971 resulted from a growing dissatisfaction with voluntary reform and a return to the idea of providing incentives for individuals (unfair dismissal) and unions (the immunities and benefits provided by registration) in exchange for the conduct of relationships within a framework of law.

Rising inflation and rising unemployment

At the same time, events emanating from changed economic circumstances were beginning to alter the way in which manpower and industrial relations problems needed to be approached. The background of the 1970s became one of persistently rising unemployment, a trend which can be traced back to 1967. From an unemployment level of a little above two and a half per cent 10 years before, it rose to more than six per cent in 1977 and 1978. At the same time inflation reached unprecedented levels and confounded the conventional economic theory of the 1950s and 1960s which suggested that a rise in the level of unemployment would reduce inflation by dampening aggregate demand.[24] The high levels of inflation led to restrictive national economic policies, particularly substantial cutbacks in public expenditure. Moreover the sharp increases in oil prices in 1973 had deflationary effects on the world economy since the increased revenues by OPEC countries did not result in an equivalent increase in expenditure in world markets by those countries concerned. The net result was a recession in world trade with rising unemployment in virtually every Western country and a reluctance on the part of any one nation to expand their own economy for fear of further inflation or balance of payments difficulties.

In Britain, as elsewhere, government policies and legislation have been aimed at alleviating the twin problems of rising unemployment and inflation. A central tenet of anti-inflationary policy has been incomes policy, although monetary and price control have been part of the package. The main problem in running an incomes policy has been to secure the compliance of the unions. The 'Social Contract' which was developed between the incoming Labour Government and the TUC in 1974 was, effectively, such an attempt. The 'Contract' required the TUC for its part to use its influence amongst affiliated unions to assist the Government in securing moderate wage settlements. The Government for its part would abolish the Industrial Relations Act, introduce subsidies on food and rent to enhance the 'social wage' and introduce a package of social legislation to enhance the rights of employees at work. This package was to include more rigorous control of health and safety, tighter controls on unfair dismissal, rights to lay-off pay, paid leave during pregnancy and legislation against race and sex discrimination. Of course much of this legislation was seen as socially necessary in a modern industrial state and also served to bring Britain into line with the practice of many of our European partners, but it clearly also served the function of trying to create an atmosphere conducive to wage restraint.

The other important area of policy development was in the manpower field. In response to the criticism which emerged in the early 1970s that there was a need to co-ordinate national manpower and employment policies, particularly the need to retrain workers being made redundant in declining industries and redeploy them in expanding ones, the Manpower Services Commission was established in 1974 with training and employment branches, the latter taking over the Department of Employment's responsibility for running the public employment service. At the same time, with unemployment growing, there was a shift in the emphasis of manpower policies. Although the Redundancy Payments Act remained on the statute book, there was less emphasis on 'shaking out' labour than under full employment. The range of measures introduced in 1975 and 1976, including the Job Creation Programme, the Work Experience Programme and Youth Employment Subsidy, were aimed at providing work and work experience for the growing number of young unemployed. These measures were extended in 1978 under the Special Temporary Employment Programme and the Youth Opportunities Programme. Besides direct Government financial support to assist ailing industries and preserve employment, a Temporary

Employment Subsidy has been paid in a number of industries to avoid redundancies. This scheme was introduced in 1975 with the objective of deferring redundancies of 10 or more workers by offering a weekly subsidy, payable for a maximum of 12 months, for each full-time job maintained. About three-fifths of all these payments have gone to protect jobs in the textile, clothing and footwear industries.

A Small Firms Employment Subsidy also became available to manufacturing firms of 200 employees or less in 'assisted areas', the subsidy being provided for each extra new job created. Between the introduction of the first measures in April 1975 and the end of 1977, 600,000 workers were reckoned to have benefited, more than half of these (370,000) under the Temporary Employment Subsidy. In 1977 alone, these measures reduced registered unemployment by over 200,000.

Given persistent or increased levels of unemployment in the future, there seems little doubt that governments will continue to develop manpower policy with the objective of alleviating unemployment. Indeed, our review of the role of government in the manpower and industrial relations fields over the last three decades provides evidence of an ever deepening involvement. The increasing complexity of the economy, persistent economic difficulties, and the government's key position as the largest employer indicate that its role as legislator and interested third party have become a permanent feature of industrial life.

2

Social change
and attitudes to work

Having looked at the effect of changing economic fortunes on the industrial relations system, it is worth pausing to consider changing social attitudes, particularly in relation to work. It is undoubtedly a widely held view amongst those with many years of experience in industry that the last two or three decades have witnessed significant changes in attitudes to work. Since this area of attitude measurement, particularly when referring to a large segment of the workforce, is fraught with both technical difficulties and problems of subjectivity, there may be a tendency for views to be general and impressionistic.

A major source of change may be found in the economic environment created after 1945. The arrival of full employment, the welfare state, greater educational opportunities and rapidly rising living standards – all those features referred to in the 1950s as 'The Affluent Society' – raised aspirations and expectations in sections of society which had not enjoyed these privileges in the past. Full employment led employees to believe that they had security for life at the workplace. Moreover, regular wage increases and an expanding market in consumer durables led the employee to expect more in the coming year than in the last. Zweig referred to this as 'the revolution of rising expectations' and said of the average worker that:

> His appetite is whetted, he wants more. He has a good life but he wants more of it . . . (and) linked with this is the steep rise in acquisitive instincts.[25]

At the same time the post-war expansion in education not only led to a generally better-educated workforce, but the teaching methods adopted led to a qualitative change in attitudes on the part of the new generation coming through the school system. In particular, more emphasis was placed on individual development and the need to question; less on obedience and conformity.

A number of effects of these changes may be observed. Reference has already been made to the effect of full employment on trade union bargaining power at the workplace. But undoubtedly social and educational change played a part in this process which Flanders once termed 'the challenge from below.'[26] Not only did the tight labour market and reduced threat of unemployment increase the power of workplace bargaining but also social and educational changes produced the confidence to challenge managerial decision-making. This found expression in the growing number of shop-stewards who increasingly took on a bargaining role almost independent of the official trade union structure. One study of the Engineering Union suggested that in that union they increased by about 50 per cent between 1947 and 1961.[27] This development was all the more interesting since most union rule books until the late 1960s made no provision for this role, although with the rise of such leaders as Jack Jones (Transport Workers) and Hugh Scanlon (Engineering) in the 1960s who were committed to shop floor democracy within trade unions, amendments were made to take account of these changes. Unions themselves became major vehicles for maintaining rising expectations and rising standards of living. During the period of rising living standards in the 1950s and early 1960s, membership of trade unions declined slightly from 45 to 42 per cent of the labour force. In the last 10 years, when inflation and a reduction to the growth of living standards began to adversely affect aspirations, union membership has grown to over 12 million or about 52 per cent of the labour force.[28]

Within the debate on motivation, the social and economic change of the post-war period has also been significant. One influential approach has been that of Maslow.[29] He has suggested that motivation should be seen in terms of a hierarchy of human needs and only with the satisfaction of a lower need would the individual be motivated by the next need in the hierarchy. In order from lowest to highest, the needs identified were physiological, safety and security, social, ego and status, and finally self-actualization or self-fulfilment. Its relationship to the 'affluent society' can be seen. Full employment, economic growth and the welfare state provided the basic needs. Physiological needs, food, drink and general sustenance, security, jobs and homes and to some extent social needs were met largely by the new economic framework. Thus the challenge to employers was to meet the higher needs, status and self-fulfilment in the jobs they provided. Maslow's theory influenced the widely known writings of Herzberg[30] and McGregor.[31] For Herzberg the higher needs became motivators, achievement, recognition, responsibility, advancement, growth, the content of the work itself, requiring a reanalysis of the content of jobs to provide 'job enrichment'. For McGregor they became 'Theory Y', the development of individual talents and creativity in meeting organizational objectives.

Thus, economic, social and educational change raised expectations amongst employees. They expected higher extrinsic rewards, security of employment, more say in matters which affected them and jobs which matched their rising educational attainments.

Part two

TODAY AND TOMORROW

3

The changing labour market

Many of the problems facing our economy up to the present time, which have been highlighted in the previous two chapters, provide a framework for understanding the national policies pursued. Many of them focussed on a new and developing role for the personnel function and this section aims to identify currently developing trends facing the personnel specialist during the next few years. Some of the problems are familiar and recurring. Many are new and challenge assumptions underlying past practice, requiring a new approach to their solution. What then are these problems?

Employment and unemployment

As discussed in the previous section, the 20 year period from the late 1940s to the late 1960s was characterized by the familiar pattern of cyclical unemployment which, although subject to regional fluctuations, averaged two and a half per cent or less in the country as a whole. In the 1970s unemployment has shown a marked tendency to increase sharply, never falling to the levels experienced in the two post-war decades and peaked in 1977 to over six per cent (*see* Table 1, page 28).

The rising trend in unemployment tells only part of the story. The graph on page 29 plots the growth of the total working population between 1950–78 against the employed labour force, the gap between the lines indicating unemployment. Between 1950–66 the total working population increased by just over two million, but in that period the economy similarly generated over two million new jobs, indeed the figure is larger than this when allowance is made for the reduction in the size of the armed forces from the early 1950s onwards. From the late 1960s onwards, an unemployment gap tended to widen between those seeking work and those employed to the extent that the employed labour force today is smaller than it was in the mid 1960s.

Table 1*
UK Unemployment Act 1950–78

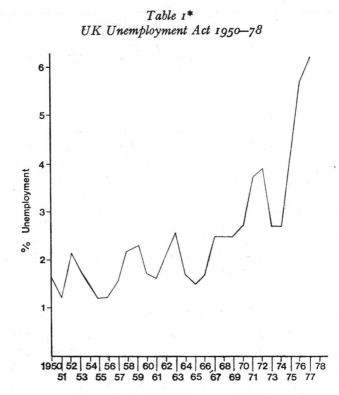

Four groups of people in the labour market have been particularly severely hit by this rise in unemployment. First, young people have been adversely affected because, with rising unemployment, their relative lack of work experience makes them a less attractive employment proposition when employers are able to recruit experienced employees from the pool of the unemployed. The Manpower Services Commission note that unemployment among young people (16 and 17 year olds) rose by 120 per cent between January 1972 and January 1977, while unemployment in the workforce as a whole rose by 45 per cent

*Data sources for tables follow the references on page 155
28

in this same period.[32] Secondly, the general rise in unemployment
has particularly affected ethnic minority groups. To see the
impact of this, when unemployment rose between 1974–77 by
120 per cent, unemployment amongst coloured workers increased
by 350 per cent.[33] Thirdly, rising unemployment tends to affect
the older worker more severely. In January 1978 for example,
more than a fifth of long term unemployed men were in the age
group of 60 and over and the median length of unemployment
within this age group increased from nearly 13 weeks to 57 weeks
between January 1971 and January 1978, against a median
national increase of 11 to nearly 22 weeks in the same period.[34]
Fourthly, a general rise in unemployment has adversely affected
registered disabled who, even under full employment, suffer
higher rates of unemployment.

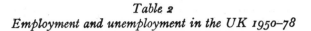

Table 2
Employment and unemployment in the UK 1950–78

Given this underlying trend of rising unemployment, what are the
likely future trends? The chart on page 30 indicates some of the
projections of unemployment levels in the UK over the next
decade.

Before looking more closely at these projections, a word of caution needs to be entered into. As one noted analyst of the labour market recently wrote:

> Projections of this kind are always fraught with difficulties, and we do not pretend ... that they can be done with any absolute accuracy.[35]

Projections of unemployment levels, as with all projections and forecasts, must be based on a set of assumptions. In some cases there can be almost absolute certainty about what will happen, in other cases there can be reasonable certainty, but in some guesswork (albeit intuitive) must be deployed. Elements of all these are present in these projections and the final outcome will be affected by economic growth, labour productivity, technical change, government policy and other changes, the effects of which can substantially affect the basis of assumptions.

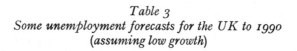

Table 3
Some unemployment forecasts for the UK to 1990
(assuming low growth)

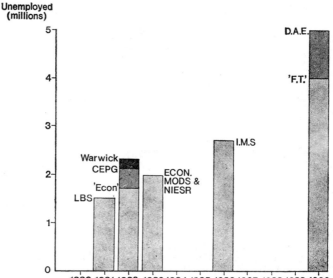

Nevertheless, the projection based on clearly-stated assumptions is an invaluable tool for planning policy at all levels in the economy, from government to individual organization. Moreover, the variety of projections considered here come to relatively similar conclusions. Based on the assumption that levels of economic growth will continue to increase at the rate of two and a half per cent per annum (as has been the tendency over the very long term in the UK), all projections point to a growing number of unemployed people. The overall picture is one of unemployment around the two million level in the early 1980s, growing towards two and a half million by the middle of the decade, and those who look ahead to the end of the decade see substantially higher levels than those of the early 1980s.

Some of the reasons underlying these projections will be discussed in the following sections.

Economic growth and productivity

The term 'economic growth' refers to the annual rate of increase in a country's real gross national product, which is the monetary value of all goods and services produced by an economy in a year. Thus a growth in the national production of goods and services is a major means of raising general living standards and providing employment.

Long term growth in the UK during the whole of this century has averaged about two and a half per cent a year. The period from the mid 1950s to mid 1960s was exceptional, with growth averaging 3.1 per cent a year, perhaps reflecting the particularly favourable conditions for the expansion of trade in the world at this time.[36] In the following decade to the mid 1970s this average fell to just above two per cent a year. The table on page 32 gives some indication of UK growth performance in relation to other countries.

Although bearing in mind the reservation that these figures are influenced by the level of economic development at the *beginning* of the period in question, particularly in the case of Japan, the conclusion cannot be avoided that the UK has tended to achieve economic growth rates below those of comparable countries and speculation as to why this should be has already been referred to. Looking at growth in GDP for a more recent period, 1973–77, Japan grew by nearly 13 per cent, France, USA and Italy above eight per cent, West Germany by nearly six per cent and Britain by 0.1 per cent.[37]

Prognostications about future growth trends, based on the past experience, cannot be optimistic. Six years ago, Lord Rothschild, then head of the think tank warned that Britain's domestic product might be only half that of West Germany and France by 1985[38] and about the same time the *Hudson Report* predicted a continuation of low growth rates for the UK into the 1980s.[39] Very little has occurred since this time, either in the domestic or international economic environment, to suggest that the UK's low rates of economic growth, with its consequent pressures of unemployment, will not persist during the next few years.

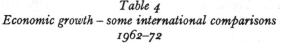

Table 4
Economic growth – some international comparisons
1962–72

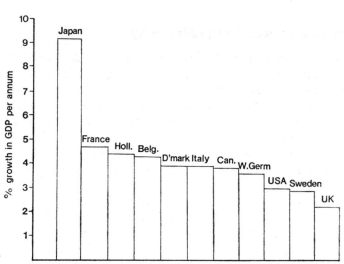

Labour productivity, that is output per person, is a frequently used although often a difficult-to-measure statistic of the efficient use of capital and labour and ultimately industrial competitiveness. Although the emphasis is output per *person*, the human element is only part of the ratio. Other critical elements include the level of investment in new plant, machinery or equipment, the general level of demand in the economy, and the efficiency of the organizational structure itself, to name but a few variables. Moreover, the productivity of many jobs is difficult to measure, particularly those which are involved with giving services or advice rather than producing goods.

Despite these problems, productivity is nevertheless a frequently used measure. Ray has noted that

32

Compared to previous rates, the growth of UK productivity since 1945 has been rapid, but it has been slower than that of comparable countries.[40]

Research by the Department of Employment indicates the levels of increase in productivity in Britain in the post-war period are as follows:[41]

	1954–63	*1963–73*	*1954–73*
Manufacturing	+2.8%	+4.2%	+3.5%

	1950–61	*1961–71*	*1950–71*
Retail distribution	+0.8%	+2.2%	+1.5%

Productivity increased in both sectors, with an acceleration in the latter period compared with the former, which was more marked in manufacturing. The picture in the more recent period 1973–77 has been somewhat different with a growth of output per person in Britain of plus 1.3 per cent which, although above the USA's increase of 0.1 per cent, was below that of Italy (2.7 per cent), Japan (7.2 per cent), France (9.4 per cent) and West Germany (10.1 per cent) in this same period.[42] As regards future trends, Ray has offered a number of scenarios which indicate that future productivity rates are subject to many intervening variables. What is most striking is that if UK rates of productivity were to reach those of the EEC, unemployment in the UK could reach 16 per cent.[43]

Both economic growth and increased productivity have important effects on industrial competitiveness and employment. Low rates of economic growth with some growth in productivity, which one might expect through the adoption of new technology, mean further pressures on the job market.

The growth of the labour force

The growth of the labour force results from a complex interplay of demographic, social, political and cultural factors. The diagram on page 34 indicates how the labour force has grown since 1951 and how it is projected to grow to 1986. Between 1951 and 1971 the workforce increased from roughly 22½ to 25 million, an increase of about 10 per cent which was very much in line with the increase in the population of the country as a whole. During the period 1971–86, however, when the total population is expected to remain virtually static at just under 56 million, the size of the labour force is expected to increase by 11 per cent from 25 million in 1971 to 27¾ million in 1986. The demographic factors bringing about this change are considered below.

Table 5
Growth of the labour force 1951–86

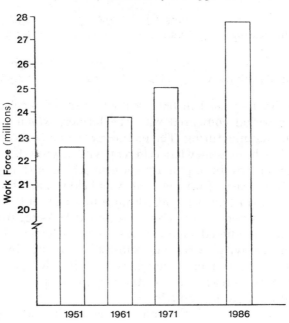

Women at work

The diagram on page 35 shows clearly what has happened in the post-war period. The total number of men in the labour force increased little, from just over 15½ million in 1951 to a projected 16½ million in 1986. Much of the increase in the labour force during this period can be explained by the increased participation of women. In 1950, women as a whole constituted 31 per cent of the total labour force and this proportion is expected to rise to 40 per cent by 1986. Even more significant within this overall change has been the increase in the number of married women going out to work: this number is expected to have almost trebled between 1951–86 from 2½ to 7½ million. The net effect is that in the mid 1980s, 40 per cent of the total labour force will be women,

34

over two-thirds of whom will be married, and it is this group which will account for the bulk of the increase in the labour force between 1971–86.

Table 6
Growth of the labour force: men and women 1951–86

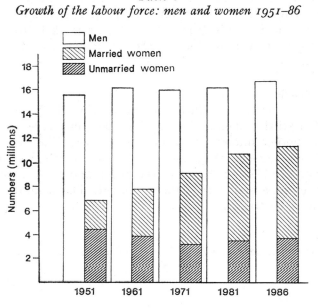

The reasons for the increased 'activity rates' of married women may be explained in a number of ways. Birth rates, after peaking between 1955 and 1964, began to fall from about 1965 with a more rapid fall in the 1970s, leaving many more women available for employment. Legislation such as the Equal Pay Act (1970) and the Sex Discrimination Act (1975) may have encouraged more women to work, attracted by relatively higher levels of pay and opportunities. Social change, particularly the desire for higher living standards and material possessions and the generally rising aspirations emerging from educational change (as described earlier) have promoted the participation of married women in the labour market. Associated with this may have been the conscious planning of smaller families enabling women to be continuously available for employment over a period of 20 to 30 years. Finally, the growth of service sector employment and part-time working since the war are key changes without which the growth of female participation might well have been constrained. These are referred to again in a later section.

35

Whatever the explanations, married women have become an increasingly significant part of the labour force. Currently about half the married women in Britain are economically active. There is some uncertainty about future trends in the activity rates of married women, but it is thought that these will rise, but less steeply than in the immediate past. If trends in Sweden are any indicator, this group of employees is likely to expand further. Currently in Sweden some 80 per cent of married mothers go out to work.

Young people
Changes in birth rates have not only affected the participation of married women in the labour market, but have also given rise to another important demographic effect. The increase in birth rates between 1955 and 1964 is swelling the numbers of young people leaving school in the 1970s and early 1980s and consequently entering the labour market. The diagram below illustrates the trends.

Table 7
Growth of young people (16–19 years) in the labour market
1971–86

From the low point in 1974, there are expected to be over 300,000 more young people between 16 to 19 years of age in the labour market by the peak year 1981. After this date the falling birth rates from the mid 1960s onwards will be reflected in a fall in the numbers of young people in this age group in the labour market.

Retirement rates
During the early 1980s the numbers who will be reaching pensionable age (men aged 65 and over and women aged 60 and over) will be below average because of the low birth rates during and immediately after the 1914–18 war. As a result not only will more people be entering the labour market at this time but also fewer people than average will be leaving it.

For a variety of reasons including cultural, social and demographic, there will be a sharp increase during the next few years in the numbers of people actively seeking employment.

Industrial structure

Industrial activity may be divided into three major sectors. Primary industries have to do with the production of raw materials and food and include agriculture, forestry, fishing, mining and quarrying. Secondary industries are concerned with the production of goods and include manufacturing industries, construction and the public utilities, gas, electricity and water. The tertiary or service sector includes the whole range of services provided by the public and private sectors: transport, communications, health, education, banking, insurance, hotels, catering, public administration and professional services. The diagram on page 38 indicates how employment has shifted between these three sectors in the British economy in the post-war-period.

The proportion of the workforce employed in manufacturing has shown a long term tendency to decline, which follows the pattern which has been occurring in the primary sector since the late nineteenth century. In the early 1800s, the working population was equally divided between the three sectors. Throughout the nineteenth century employment decreased in the primary sector and increased in both the secondary and service sector. As long ago as the early years following the Industrial Revolution, a substantial proportion of the working population was employed in services, and it was in the late nineteenth century that the expansion of employment in the secondary sector slowed up, but continued to grow in the service sector. Thus, while the service sector has for long been a substantial employer of labour in Britain, its expansion has been particularly rapid in the post-war period and is expected to employ 57 per cent of the working population in 1981 as against 47 per cent in 1951.

Table 8
Employment by industrial sector 1951–81

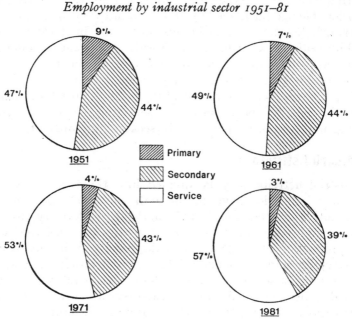

The recent short-run shifts in the sectoral distribution of employment are highlighted by looking at inter-industry changes in employment between 1961–81 in the table on page 39, focussing on both growing and declining industries.

The role of the service sector in providing an expansion of employment in this period is clearly emphasized, with marked growth in public services (particularly education and health), private services, banking and insurance. The declining industries in terms of employment largely represent the traditional manufacturing base of British industry which has been in decline over a long period of time. A number of underlying reasons for these shifts may be noted. First, new technology has brought about increased output with a reduced labour force. Secondly, the reorganization of an industry through mergers and economies of scale has reduced the demand for labour. Thirdly, demand for

38

certain products fell as a result of a change in tastes or the inability of the industry to produce at a quality or price at which people will buy. Fourthly, the exhaustion of a natural resource brought about the decline of an industry based upon that resource (the position of some primary extractive industries).

Table 9
Inter-industry changes in employment 1961–81

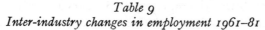

A particular cause of declining employment in manufacturing in the UK and the older industrial nations has been the shift of a great deal of manufacturing industry to the newly developing nations. This trend has been facilitated by the relative lack of technological sophistication in many of these industries, together with rapidly rising labour costs in Europe, making the goods produced by the latter less cost competitive. Amongst the declining industries listed above, clothing, textiles and to some extent shipbuilding can be explained in this way. Moreover in the UK these difficulties have been further aggravated because British industry has not been able to compete effectively in the growth industry of high technology, much of which is imported.

39

The growth in service industries also reflects the new and growing demands of the more affluent consumer. He or she demands improvements in the quality of life (health, education and social services) and has more leisure time and greater income to spend on the services offered by this sector – restaurants, entertainments, sport, travel, tourism and so on.

The shift towards employment in services and away from manufacturing should not be seen as a purely British phenomenon. The USA became the world's first 'service economy' in the 1950s, with a majority of the workforce in the service sector. Since then, Canada, Belgium, the Netherlands, Sweden, Switzerland and the UK have experienced similar developments. Daniel Bell has described this as *The Coming of Post-industrial Society*.[44] The post-industrial society is seen as part of a 'maturing' process going on within industrial societies. As formerly underdeveloped economies industrialize, so currently developed societies move into post-industrialism. Such societies have small, highly capital-intensive and automated manufacturing sectors generally producing technologically sophisticated, high quality goods, with a large proportion of employment in the service sector either selling and exporting services – banking, insurance, advice, designs or other professional services – or expanding social services and facilities related to an improvement in the quality of life – health, education, recreation and culture. Already USA, Japan, Canada, Scandinavia, Switzerland, France, West Germany and the Benelux countries have been described as 'visibly post-industrial', while the UK, USSR, Italy, Austria, East Germany, Czechoslovakia, Israel, Australia and New Zealand have been termed 'early post-industrial'.[45]

This kind of analytical framework is helpful in trying to understand the changing industrial structure and will be referred to again when examining other aspects of our changing environment.

Occupational structure

Change in the occupational structure is clearly related to changes in the industrial structure – occupations performed by people reflect the skills demanded by industry and changes in the relative size of industry. As illustrated on page 41, a shift away from primary and manufacturing employment leads to a decline in the demand for manual skills and a shift towards the service

40

sector tends to lead to an increase in the demand for non-manual skills. The last decade has witnessed, for the first time in Britain,

Table 10
Changing occupational structure 1951–81

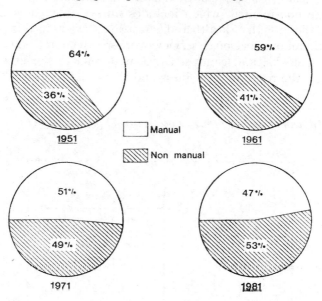

the employment of more non-manual rather than manual employees in the workforce. But, as with the switch to service sector employment discussed above, this is a development observed in many countries and reflects the development of post-industrialism. Since post-industrialism involves automation, high technology and a large service sector, so a decline in the demand for manual skills and growth in non-manual would be expected to emerge from these developments. The danger to the British economy comes from our slow and patchy adoption of high technology without which sufficient added value to sustain the increase in services cannot be produced.

The table on page 42 indicates the past and future impact of these changes on the growth or decline of the major occupational groups between 1961 and 1981.

The shift to service sector employment, the changes in technology and the changing scale of industrial enterprises are reflected in these changes. The growth of the large-scale enterprise and its increased technical and organizational problems are reflected in the increased numbers of managers, professional specialists (including engineers and scientists), technical (intermediate non-manual) and clerical and sales (junior non-manual) personnel. The two occupational groups with the largest growth, professional (which includes doctors and dentists) and intermediate non-manual (which includes nurses and teachers) also reflect the growth of health and education services in this period. Growth among personal service workers (who include housekeepers, cooks, and canteen assistants) reflects the growth of tourism, the restaurant business and the social services.

Table 11
Growth or decline of major occupational groupings 1961–81

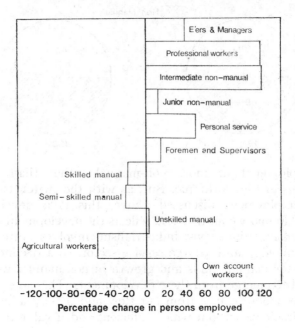

Percentage change in persons employed

Amongst manual workers, there is a static or declining situation which interestingly coincides with a growth of 15 per cent in the number of foremen and supervisors of manual employees. Perhaps surprisingly, despite technological advance and automation, the demand for unskilled manual workers will change little, while the skilled and semi-skilled occupational groups will decline significantly.

42

Other changing patterns of employment

Over and above the changes already described, a number of other developments in the labour market are worth noting since they have important implications for employment policies.

Part-time working

It has already been noted that women, particularly married women, have been going out to work in increasing numbers. Between 1951 and 1971, women increased from 31 per cent to 37 per cent of the total labour force and much of this increase can be accounted for by an increase in part-time working during that period. The table below indicates how part-time working amongst women has accounted for an increasing proportion of all female employment.[46]

Table 12
Part-time female employees as a percentage of all female employees
1951–76

	1951	1961	1971	1975
Manufacturing	12.2	13.7	18.7	24.2
All industries	N/A	25.0	33.5	39.5

Research by the Department of Employment into the characteristics of part time female employees indicated that most were over 35 and married with small families. The majority worked in service industries (professional and scientific services, distribution, banking, insurance and public administration) and were largely engaged in catering, domestic and service occupations, and office work.[47]

Research by Leicester suggests that part-time working is likely to increase in the future with the increase in number of employees in part-time employment exceeding the increase in growth of the labour force. The number of part-time employees by the end of the century could exceed seven million as against four million currently and part-timers would therefore account in the future for about a quarter of the employed labour force. While part-time working has, in the past, been a feature of women's employment, it might in the future become a feature of the employment of men also.[48]

Temporary work

Although precise figures are not available, evidence would suggest that temporary employment has mushroomed in growth in the last 15 years. This is probably symptomatic of rising labour costs and its associated overheads, the increased difficulties of 'hiring and firing' and an aspect of what Alvin Toffler has termed 'the rental revolution', in which the pace of change and its accompanying obsolescence make it more advantageous to rent or hire than to buy.[49] Formerly temporary work had been a feature of industries which experienced marked seasonal changes in demand (such as agriculture or hotels and catering), but during the last decade it has developed amongst such occupations as nursing, draughtsmen, drawing office staff, clerks, secretaries and construction workers.[50]

Although still relatively small in number as a proportion of the whole labour force, temporary employment is likely to have a continuing influence on the labour market.

The black labour market

Interest has risen in the 'black labour market', otherwise known as 'moonlighting' or double job holding. Although information on this labour market is scant, continued skill shortages or the shorter or more flexible working week could encourage more participation in such secondary occupations. In view also of the growth of part-time working, double jobholders could increasingly become a key component in manpower supply.

Age of the labour force

The table below indicates some broad shifts taking place in the age structure of the labour force.

Table 13
Age of the labour force – percentage in each age group 1971–1986

Year/Age	16–24	25–44	45–65
1971	20	39	41
1986	20	45	35

As a result of demographic trends, the labour force in the 1980s will be comparatively younger than in the 1970s and indeed

44

younger than any British workforce this century. There will be an increase in the 25–44 age group accompanied by a corresponding decrease in the 45–65 age group.

4

Changing technology

In many respects, technology and technological innovation may be viewed as central components of the kind of changes described above. Technology plays a key part in economic growth by raising industrial productivity, while at the same time raising standards of living, income levels and leisure time by making possible substantially reduced working hours. This process tends to displace labour but at the same time the falling costs of production generate mass markets for new products, which in turn stimulate employment in developing industries. Technological change therefore underlies many changes in the industrial and occupational structure and, as we shall see in Chapter 10, the relationship between education and working life.

The effect of technological change on overall unemployment levels in an economy has long been a matter for debate amongst economists. Historically mechanization has had no harmful effect on employment – unprecedented levels of full employment were reached after 1945 in a period of rapid technological advance because new products or services were being demanded. Nevertheless, there seems to be an increasing number of economists, some of whose projections were referred to earlier, who are taking a pessimistic view of the future effects of technological change on employment. New developments in automated technology are felt to be sufficiently revolutionary that we shall witness the large-scale displacement of labour which will not be balanced by the number of new jobs generated by the new technology.

Leaving aside this argument for the moment, technological change has played a key role in promoting economic growth, industrial change and, as we shall see in Chapter 8, in affecting behaviour within organizations. What technological changes are foreseen for the 1980s?

A useful overview has been provided by the Manpower Services Commission (MSC) document *Training for Skills*.[51] As part of their analysis of the future skill needs of industry within a context of technical change, the Commission conducted a survey amongst 76 employers with a total employment of 3.7 million located in each of the major industrial sectors. The perceptions of senior management in relation to impact of technical change between 1977 and 1987 in each industry is illustrated below.

Table 14
Impact of technological change 1977–87

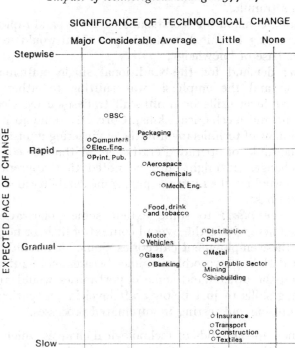

Most sectors foresaw gradual rather than rapid change with the exception of those industries—British Steel, computers, electrical engineering and printing and publishing—which were already experiencing the impact of technological change. But the MSC concluded that many respondents may have underestimated the potential impact of some aspects of technical change on their

47

organizations, particularly the effect of computer technology on the administrative, clerical and secretarial procedures within the office. The main implications of changes which employers foresaw were as follows:

Employment: a majority of sectors expected a decline in numbers employed compared to the present time, in some instances by up to 30 per cent of current numbers.

Middle management: a need was foreseen for training in a wider range of skills, not only technical arising out of changed technology, but also in increased numeracy and problem solving skills associated with operational research training, and behavioural and leadership skills associated with industrial relations training.

Technicians: demand for technicians would expand rapidly and the increasing technical demand upon them would require a broader base of knowledge.

Craftsmen: demand for the traditional single craftsman was declining and the emphasis was shifting to either higher technician-level skills or multi-skill tradesmen (eg electrical, electronic and mechanical skills). Currently some 40 per cent of the inflow of technicians into the engineering industry come from the ranks of upgraded craftsmen. Within the context of these changes, it might also be noted that apprenticeship training would in the future require some flexibility and a wider technical base.

Semi and unskilled: to some extent some polarization was expected here within the overall context of little or no growth within these employment categories. Some jobs would become further deskilled as production lines became more automated, while on the other hand some opportunities would arise for acquiring skills to just below craft level in occupations such as monitoring and testing in automated processes.

To turn now to the kinds of technological changes which can be expected in the next few years, a paper by the Department of Industry has unequivocally concluded that:

Microelectronics is likely to be the dominant technology of the next decade.[52]

Certainly given the enormous interest and debate which has recently emerged amongst government departments, employers and trade unions, together with direct government investment in the microelectronic industry through the National Enterprise Board, such a prediction may not be wide of the mark. If microelectronic technology is going to make an impact throughout British industry, it is well worth paying closer attention to what the implications of this are.

At the centre of the discussion is the computer, electronic technology and the enormous pace with which technological developments have occurred in this field in a relatively short space of time. From the invention of the transistor in 1947 (which was to devastate the valve industry), technology advanced with enormous rapidity in the electronics industry, particularly in the field of miniaturization. A technical breakthrough in the early 1960s enabled up to four transistors to be built on to one small piece of silicon and from this emerged the technical phenomenon which has entered everyday speech during the last year, the silicon chip. Recent developments in semiconductor technology have led to the manufacture of integrated circuits which now contain a quarter of a million transistors on one silicon chip only a quarter of an inch square. Predictions are that by 1985 single integrated circuit chips could contain more than 10 million elements.[53] The chip can absorb, sift, analyse and produce information in an infinite variety of ways. Several chips mounted on a card become a microprocessor and a microprocessor connected to a storage mechanism and input and output devices becomes a micro-computer. To quote recent analysts, the microprocessor 'embodies many of the capabilities of conventional large scale computers in a space smaller than a matchbox'.[54]

The effects of these developments may briefly be outlined. The major advantage is relative cheapness. As the technology advances and the market expands, prices fall while the product improves. A recent article indicated that many of the established companies in the microelectronics field are able to lower the prices of memories by 35 to 40 per cent a year[55] and the falling costs brought about by the microcomputer can be dramatically illustrated as follows – by 1980 it will be possible to purchase computer power for £7000 that would have cost one million pounds in 1965.[56] A further advantage is its smallness. Gone is the specially air-conditioned and controlled environment of the standard computer; the microcomputer can be placed on the manager's desk. Other advantages are their increased reliability and their flexibility of application.

Of major importance to personnel managers are their likely applications in industry and their effects on skills, job structures and unemployment. In many respects, 'likely' impact is a misnomer since already the impact of the chip has been felt. The Swiss watch industry was devastated by the arrival of the electronic watch from the USA. The same happened to the mechanical desk calculators, replaced by the cheap electronic pocket calculator. Both these new products are generally based on the microprocessor.

Where can we expect the microprocessor to be applied in industry? Essentially microprocessors can be used in a product itself, to extend automation on an industrial or manufacturing process or to further automate manual office procedures. Looking first at product change, the microprocessor can give rise to a completely new product, sophisticated new toys such as TV video games are a recent example, or it can radically change an old product, making it much cheaper and transforming its market – electronic watches and pocket calculators are the recent examples here. It is difficult to say what other products of these categories will come onto the market, but sceptics suggest that they may be minimal. Perhaps more important in relation to product change is the application of microprocessors to increase the sophistication of existing products without necessarily transforming their market. Here the list is longer. Microprocessors are likely to replace electro-mechanical control mechanisms in washing machines, sewing machines, ovens and other domestic household equipment, improving its performance and reliability.[57] They are also likely to be used increasingly in motor cars to perform new and sophisticated control functions. Already cars at the top end of the price range, including Mercedes, Aston-Martin Lagonda and Jensen-Healey, are incorporating this new technology. Functions which microprocessors can be expected to perform include anti-skid control, automatic ignition timing, automatic door-locking, exhaust emission control and fault diagnosis, amongst some of their applications.[58]

The major impact of the new technology is expected to be on industrial and office systems and is likely to have a significant effect on established patterns of employment and skills. It is to these problems that we shall return when examining the impact of technological change on employing organizations.

5

Changing employment law

The first chapter traced the main influences underlying the development of labour law in Britain. The traditional framework had been one of non-intervention, 'voluntarism', in which the law provided basic rights to employees at work, while the majority of issues were to be settled either by management alone or through management and trade union agreement. Governments became increasingly drawn into a more interventionist role between employers and workers for a number of reasons. The government itself became the nation's largest employer. The Keynesian economic strategy adopted after the war implicitly involved a more active role for government. Economic problems, particularly balance of payments deficits and inflation, were diagnosed as stemming from deficiencies in the structure of employer and union bargaining. Social change and rising aspirations led employees to demand more rights through legislation. Employers, comparing unfavourably the degree of legal regulation in our system of industrial relations with that of many other countries, from the 1960s urged greater legal control of trade union activities.

One or other of these pressures drew the State, and frequently the law also, into an interventionist position. In the 1960s, the law together with newly established institutions in the area of redundancy, training and industrial relations reform were aimed at raising productivity by shaking out excess manpower from organizations and encouraging the greater mobility of labour. Policies were adopted against a background of full employment and a shortage of labour, particularly skilled labour. In the 1970s, however, while the problems of manpower underutilization and skill shortage remained, the background became one of growing unemployment, particularly amongst the young. Legislation and policy measures started to emphasize job security rather than redundancy and dismissal. Under the 1971 Industrial Relations Act, the dismissal of an employee with two years service or more could be unfair. Under the Trade Union and Labour Relations Act of 1974, the concept of 'constructive' dismissal was added, (ie where the employer took action that virtually forced the resignation of the employee). Also the qualifying service for claiming unfair dismissal was reduced to 26 weeks. In the light of the trend in legislation, the appropriately named Employment Protection Act was passed in 1975 adding a range of measures to further job security. The periods of notice which had to be given to employees were extended; employees found to have been unfairly dismissed could seek reinstatement or re-engagement; specified periods of notice were required before the declaration of redundancy; redundancy itself was to become an issue for consultations with trade unions; temporary lay-offs were discouraged through guaranteed pay provisions; pregnant women were protected against dismissal and became entitled to reinstatement. This comprehensive range of measures was aimed at increasing the security of the individual against growing unemployment and at discouraging dismissal. Recent evidence supports the view that dismissals fell sharply during the 1970s.[59]

As discussed earlier also, the establishment of the Manpower Services Commission (MSC) in 1974 coincided with a new and developing role for manpower policies – the combating of unemployment. Thus labour subsidies, such as the Temporary Employment Subsidy, and a whole range of job creation and work experience measures were introduced either to discourage redundancies or otherwise reduce the number of people on the unemployment register. As one recent commentator on manpower policies in Western Europe has noted, many of these measures reflected what was contained in the EEC Directive on Employment Protection and as a result the law in Britain introduced similar constraints on dismissal and other employment protection measures which already existed within the Community.[60]

As for the future, given persisting high levels of unemployment and low rates of economic growth, there is every reason to suppose that measures to safeguard employment are likely to continue. In addition, measures to reduce the labour supply through what is called worksharing – cuts in the working week, increased holidays, reductions in the retirement age amongst others – are increasingly being debated. Legislation is less likely here and these issues will be considered later in the light of this in chapter 7.

A glance at current provision in many Western European countries suggests that pressures from this source could further extend existing employment protection legislation in the UK. In a recent review of the topic, Rubenstein has concluded that the UK still lags behind in this respect and that the 1980s will see 'further and dramatic improvements to the statutory scheme of employment protections'.[61] Some of the major measures which he highlights are as follows:

Dismissal: in the event of a dispute over the validity of dismissal with notice, dismissal may be prevented until it is upheld by the law. In Sweden, their Employment Protection Act (1974) provides for this; in the Netherlands, the approval of the Director of the District Labour Office must be obtained; in Germany, the works council can oppose dismissal until the Labour Court has ruled on its fairness.

Written notice for dismissal: currently in Britain this need only be supplied if requested by the employee; a proposal before the EEC Council of Ministers, if enacted, would require all dismissal notices to be in writing following the practice in Belgium, Denmark and France.

Informing employees of their legal rights: the requirement that the employer must by law inform employees of their legal rights to contest a dismissal is contained within an EEC draft report recommendation.

Longer minimum notice period: the UK and Ireland are at the 'bottom of the league' in this respect in Europe; Belgium, Denmark, France, Luxembourg and the Netherlands all provide for four weeks minimum notice (in Britain this applies after four years service, the current minimum is one week) and the EEC Commission favour the general extension of the four-week minimum.

Right to time off to look for a new job: currently this right is available to employees only in a redundancy situation under the Employment Protection Act. The law in Belgium and Luxembourg, and collective agreements in other EEC countries, provide such a right in any dismissal situation, a measure which has EEC Commission support.

Selection for redundancy: despite some limits to the grounds upon which candidates may be selected for redundancy in Britain (eg sex, race, trade union membership), management discretion is still relatively wide, although further restrictions may be imposed by collective agreements which will frequently relate selection for redundancy to service, the 'last in, first out' principle. Along the lines of the practice in many EEC countries and in Sweden, this principle may become embodied in the law, priority of retention in employment being given to those with longest service.

Alternative employment: EEC proposals are likely to place a wider duty on the employer to find employment within the organization, outside it, or to assist in retraining in a redundancy situation.

Re-employment of redundant workers: Holland and Sweden have a system providing priority of re-employment for redundant workers within the same organization in the same work within a specified period (in Sweden it is one year). The EEC Commission also favour such an approach.

As regards legislation on the discrimination against particular groups in the labour force in addition to current provisions against race and sex discrimination, some discussion has emerged on the topic of 'age discrimination' which might intensify if unemployment continues to adversely affect the young and older workers. Legislation in this field was enacted over a decade ago in the USA under the Age Discrimination and Employment Act (1968). Here employees in the age group 40 to 65 are protected against discrimination on the grounds of age. As a result it is unlawful for an employer to fail to recruit, select or promote on the grounds of age alone, or to include age discrimination clauses in employee specifications or job advertisements. In Britain periodic research evidence of the role of age in selection and promotion has come to light. Research by Collins suggested that about a third of job advertisements within the personnel management profession specified upper age limits of 40 or less in their advertisements and a further number of interviews during the selection process involved the criterion of an upper age limit.[62] Other research across the whole spectrum of occupations suggests that, of those vacancies specifying upper age limits, in the region of 90 per cent excluded candidates over 50, with remarkably little variation between professional, managerial, clerical and manual groups.[63] This is not of course to suggest that there are not frequently sound reasons for these limits, including health and fitness, career development, pension arrangements and salary structures, but age discrimination may well figure amongst future legislative developments.

The final area for consideration is the development of law in the field of participation and industrial democracy. The findings of the Bullock Committee of enquiry are well known and need no further attention here.[64] The real interest stems from the debate in the aftermath of the Bullock Report and the likely legislative developments in this area. As the Bullock Report pointed out, participation is not an issue which will go away, not least because the development of legislation features in the plans of the EEC Commission. Two EEC proposals are of relevance. The first is the Fifth Directive on the harmonization of company law. Although it proposes employee representation on the boards of all companies with over 500 employees, its final form will be subject to considerable debate within the Community in order to be sufficiently flexible to cater for the differing national industrial relations systems. The other proposal concerns a European Company Statute. This would apply only to those companies wishing to register as 'European Companies' and would require companies so doing to establish a Works Council and worker representation on the Supervisory Board on the lines of current practice in most Western European countries.

A major problem confronting the development of legislation along the lines of European practice in the UK is, for historical reasons, the very different framework for industrial relations which exists here. Without entering a lengthy discussion, the major differences between Britain and Western Europe are as follows. First, the existence in Britain of a strong but relatively decentralized trade union movement with considerably more power available to shop stewards to bargain at the workplace. Secondly, the existence of multi-unionism in virtually every workplace, each union requiring representation in any system of industrial democracy. Finally, the different traditions of the role of the law. In Europe it has been used to promote such institutions as works councils and worker directors, while in Britain the law had not, until recently, become involved, but rather institutions developed through the collective bargaining pressures of trade unions. To sum up, whatever legislation is proposed in Britain, attention must be paid to the historical development in

Britain of the role of trade unions and the collective bargaining process.

The keynote of legislative development on participation in Britain is likely to be 'flexibility'. The last government's post-Bullock White Paper saw the development of a Joint Representation Committee of trade unions engaging in joint discussion with senior management on company strategy.[65] Discussion would also take place on ways of developing industrial democracy and it would only be after a three or four year period that legislation would be enacted. The White Paper favoured the development of a two-tier board system with one-third employee representation on the policy board. A possible outcome could be the introduction some time in the future of enabling legislation to allow a time period for companies and unions to develop participative institutions to meet their own needs and the worker director concept may diminish as the central issue, worker directors only being appointed where the parties feel a useful purpose is served. At the same time attention will have to be paid to those groups represented in these institutions and a failure to represent any significant group, be they managerial, clerical, or manual is likely to be to the detriment of the future of any system of participation.

Before concluding this discussion of legislation on industrial democracy, a final point is worth noting. Much of the recent debate about legislation has concerned the representative institutions of industrial democracy. But by its very nature, this cannot involve the participation of each and every member of an organization. In reality, increased participation involves a whole range of measures including both representative institutions such as collective bargaining, works and company councils and also measures aimed at enhancing the involvement of individuals through briefing groups, participative management style, autonomous work groups and job redesign. Although it is not being suggested that there is any immediate likelihood of legislation in this latter area in the UK, there is a precedent in Denmark where legislation has been enacted to promote the humanization of the workplace in relation to such issues as the conditions of the workplace and the design of jobs. There are, however, new economic considerations as well as social pressures for reforms in these areas and we shall return to these in a later section (see chapter 10).

In conclusion, social change, economic difficulty and the in-

56

fluence of the European Community suggest that Britain has embarked on an irreversible policy of continued and expanding legal intervention in employment policies. The pressures of high unemployment are likely to mean continued constraints on dismissal or lay-off. The pressures of social change are likely to bring about legislation in the field of participation and greater concern for the quality of working life.

6

Changing educational output

The relationship between the educational system and industry has shown an historical tendency to become increasingly interdependent. In pre-industrial Britain, the output of the educational system, largely scholars of classics or religion, had little relevance to the output of the productive system. Following the development of industrialization, the educational system began to expand in response to the need for more literacy and numeracy amongst the workforce. An Education Act of 1870 first introduced a minimal education for all up to the age of 10, by 1914 this had been extended to 14, and under the Act of 1944 this was extended into an extensive state system of education from the age of five to fifteen. The expansion of higher education has also been profoundly affected by technical and industrial change, although the real impact, particularly on the universities, has only been felt in the last two decades. For a long time universities generally resisted involvement in studies which might be seen as vocational. But in the post-war period, with a massive expansion of public-funding of education and increasing government support for research to improve economic growth and industrial productivity, the higher education system became generally more involved in research and training for industry. Thus, as an industrial society advances and becomes more complex, so education and industry seem to be pulled closer together.

The interdependence of industry and education is highlighted by the development of what was earlier termed the 'post-industrial' society. In such a society 'knowledge' becomes of dominant importance – Drucker has coined the term 'knowledge society'.[66] The decline in the demand for manual skills and growth in the demand for technical, professional and managerial skills referred to earlier is symptomatic of this. Knowledge and competence to manage processes and systems (which include people) become increasingly important inputs to the manufacturing sector as companies innovate to remain competitive. More firms exist and more people are employed for the purpose of selling knowledge – solicitors, accountants, architects, advisers and consultants. One recent writer has argued that 'the real wealth producer in post-industrial societies is neither land nor manufacture, but 'knowledge'.[67] This is not to say that there is currently a good match between the demands of industry and educational output but a perfect match would be unattainable and also undesirable. The response by the educational system to industrial change has long been a matter of debate. The argument by educationists has long been that too strong a vocational bias in the school curriculum stultifies human growth, narrows the choice of career for the school leaver and restricts people to a very limited range of skills. Rapid technological change lends support to the view that the educational curriculum needs to become broader rather than merely respond to the narrow vocational skills of the past and also needs to recognize that knowledge in a vacuum does not prepare young people for dealing with increasingly complex tasks.

Notwithstanding this debate, the education system has shown a long term tendency to expand with industrial development and the role of knowledge is fast becoming the basis of future economic development. It is therefore worth considering the statistical evidence to support the view that educational standards are rising.

First, the figures below indicate that between 1965 and 1975 the period spent by young people in full-time education increased, particularly amongst those remaining beyond the statutory minimum leaving age.[68]

	1965	1975
% remaining beyond statutory minimum	44	58
% remaining up to age 17	14	21
% remaining to 18 +	5	7

Secondly, looking at the qualifications obtained by school leavers indicated in the table below young people gained more examination passes in this same period. The numbers of young people obtaining no examination pass fell from 59 per cent in 1965 to

47 per cent in 1975 and in each of the other categories the number of passes obtained increased during this period.

Table 15
Qualifications of school leavers 1965 and 1975

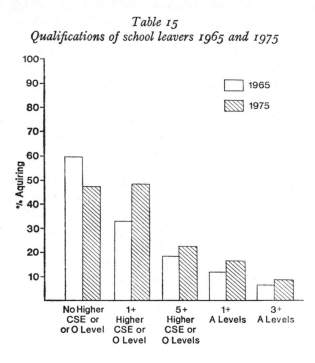

Finally, looking at past trends and projections for the future, increasing proportions of young people are undertaking all or part of a sixth-form curriculum. By 1991, it is expected that one school leaver in three will have undertaken one year of a sixth-form curriculum and more than one in five will have completed two or more years.[69] As regards projections of examinations passed, modest increases are expected amongst those achieving 'A' level passes during the 1980s and a modest fall in those obtaining little or no examination success.[70]

Before looking at the output from the higher education system, it is worth including a 'caveat' regarding these statistics of school leavers. Whilst not denying the clearly observable statistical trends indicating greater academic attainment (particularly examination passes) on the part of school leavers, many employers nevertheless remain critical. A fairly widespread view is that many school leavers applying for jobs lack the basic skills of reading, writing and arithmetic. Whilst accepting that the standards of the more able school leavers are higher than before, there is also a feeling among many employers that some polarization has occurred and that changes in the structure of employment make some of them more difficult to employ than their counterparts in the past. Although there appears to be no systematic evidence to substantiate this viewpoint, it is sufficiently widespread to be noted in any analysis of the changing output from the educational system and is an area worthy of further examination.

Turning now to the Further Education sector, the picture is again one of rapid expansion. The table below illustrates the growth in the full-time student population and indicates the extent to which this is likely to develop further during the next decade.

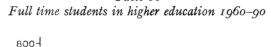

Table 16
Full time students in higher education 1960–90

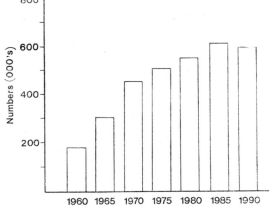

The enormous expansion during the 1960s raised the participation rate of 18 year olds in full-time education from 7 per cent in 1960 to 14 per cent by 1970.[71] The rate of increase in student numbers has tended to slow relatively in the 1970s, but nevertheless total numbers are expected to go on increasing up to the mid 1980s. After this numbers are expected to level out and then fall slightly as a result of the decline in the birth rate from the mid 1960s referred to earlier.

The period from 1960 has also been characterized by an enormous expansion in day-release, block-release and evening study not accounted for above. Between 1965 and 1975 the total number of students undertaking study by this method increased by over three-quarters of a million to nearly 3.7 million.[72] Given the cost effectiveness of this form of study both for employers, students and the public finances, there is no reason to suppose that expansion will not continue in this area.

Before moving on from the Higher Education sector, it is worth highlighting the output of highly qualified people: those with first degrees or equivalent professional qualifications, who form only a relatively small proportion of all those students in Higher Education described above. The table below indicates the trends and projections for 1971–86.

Table 17
Output of first degree graduates 1971–86

From an annual output of around 20,000 students per year in the 1950s, the figure passed 60,000 in the early 1970s and is projected to increase by almost twice to 114,000 by 1986. This rate of expansion is much swifter than that for student numbers as a whole during 1971–86. Perhaps less comprehensibly, the proportion of science graduates is expected to fall during this period, social studies to rise and arts graduates to remain about the same.

In conclusion, the educational level of the workforce is generally rising and this, coupled with our previous discussion of rising aspirations, the changing ethos emerging within the educational system and the wider framework of technical change, makes education an area with significant implications for managers and their organizations. It is therefore a theme we shall return to in the next part.

The argument so far

The many aspects of change in the social, economic and technical environment facing organizations currently and in the near future may be grouped in the following way:

The impact of persisting high unemployment: there are a number of indicators which suggest that the current high levels of unemployment are unlikely to diminish. Critical factors are lower rates of economic growth than those experienced during the 1950s and 1960s, the growth in the size of the labour force and technological change reducing employers' demand for labour.

The increasing pace of technological change: any acceleration of the pace of technological change, as suggested by new developments in microelectronic computer technology, will have profound effects on the structure of organizations, their ability to adapt to change and the nature of the skills required of the workforce. The ability of organizations to adapt to change has been a much discussed theme but nevertheless remains of critical importance.

The continuing legal regulation of employment: for reasons discussed in the first two parts, there is little evidence to suggest that the growth of statutory regulations which occurred in the 1960s and 1970s will be significantly reversed. Particularly, the pressures of high unemployment will continue to mean that dismissal and lay-off will be subject to legal constraint, and social pressures for participation may find some expression in a statute.

The rising level of attainment within the education system: longer time periods spent in full-time education and the rising educa-

64

tional attainment of an increasing number of entrants to the labour force have important implications for the structure of work as well as the aspirations and the expectations of young people at work.

All these changes have important implications for the management of human resources and are likely to raise new problems requiring a reappraisal of long-cherished practices and beliefs. The next part will consider each of these major change areas and ways in which they are likely to affect organizations.

Part three

SOME MAJOR ISSUES FOR
ORGANIZATIONS

7

Unemployment and worksharing

Reference has already been made to one very important impact
of rising unemployment on organizations – the development of
laws which tend to discourage dismissal and redundancy. The
further implications of this will be considered in chapter 9.
Another aspect of rising unemployment to which we have also
already alluded is the increasing use of labour subsidies to keep
people at work. The subsidies paid by the government have taken
a wide variety of forms (see appendix I, page 139) but have been
mainly aimed at the problems of the young unemployed and
regional or structural unemployment. A considerable debate
surrounds the use of such subsidies. Against them is the argument that they subsidise inefficiency, prop up industries which
should be run down, promote unfair competition with employers
not receiving subsidies and in short distort market forces and in
the long run endanger jobs. In favour of subsidies are the effects
on the social fabric of society of large-scale unemployment (for
example a rise in crime) and the fact that the financial cost of
providing subsidies may be no higher than the total cost of unemployment and social security benefits together with the loss
of revenue from income tax and national insurance contributions.[73] While the debate over the use of labour subsidies is
likely to continue, the use of them is understandable given the
social problems which rising unemployment throws up in the
short term. Nevertheless they contribute nothing to the longer-
term restructuring of industry upon which future employment
and prosperity must depend.

Notwithstanding these existing pressures on organizations,
there is another set of ideas emerging which are also becoming
increasingly influential amongst those seeking to alleviate the

problem of rising unemployment and which could, if adopted, have a substantial impact on many aspects of organizations. These measures may be grouped together under the heading of worksharing, the general objective of which is to 'redistribute the total volume of work in the economy in order to increase employment opportunities for all those wishing to work'.[74] Our general definition is broad, intentionally so, in order that we can consider the whole range of measures being proposed.

Pressure for further consideration and implementation of worksharing is emanating from trade unions, not only in Britain but also in other countries in Western Europe. It has also attracted the attention of the Commission of the EEC to the extent that one recent commentator has taken the view that the EEC has no alternative but to include worksharing as one element within an overall economic strategy.[75]

Worksharing measures may be divided into two groups. First, there are measures aimed at reducing the time spent at work by the existing employed labour force. The proposals here are for a reduction in the standard working week, reductions in overtime, perhaps allied to the extension of shiftwork, increased annual holidays and the extension of flexible working arrangements such as part-time working or jobsharing. Secondly, there are measures which are aimed at reducing the numbers of people actively participating in the labour market. Such measures would include early retirement, a longer period spent in education and training, and periodic sabbatical or study leave. The objective of all these measures would be to spread the jobs available across the labour force and reduce the pool of unemployed. These are the objectives, but a closer examination of each of the proposals will indicate their likely effectiveness and problems associated with them.

Reduced standard working week

It has been remarked of the American industrial relations there that 'reducing worktime, increasing leisure and related job security demands show strong indications of remaining powerful forces for quite some time'.[76] This is undoubtedly also true of Britain and elsewhere where a reduced standard working week is (and for a very long time has been) a major objective of trade unions.

Looking back over a long period of time, normal weekly

working hours have fallen substantially. At the beginning of the nineteenth century the working week frequently exceeded 70 hours, but this was gradually reduced in various industrial sectors as a result of trade union pressure. A century ago the working week was still in the region of 55-60 hours, but began to fall sharply after the turn of the century, particularly in 1918-19 when the 47 or 48 hour week became widespread. The most recent cuts in the standard working week for manual workers occurred between 1959 and 1961, when basic hours fell from 44 to 42 and between 1964 and 1966 when there was a further general fall from 42 to 40.

The long term fall in hours has been facilitated by increased efficiency and productivity brought about by technical change in industry. But hours of work, rather than falling steadily and progressively, have tended to fall sharply in a particular one or two year period, followed by a longer period of relatively little change. Clegg has suggested that these sudden falls can be attributed to the collective bargaining activities of trade unions.[77] Generally, the initial drive for a reduction in hours comes from a resolution at the TUC, is included in successive collective bargaining claims and when it is finally conceded by employers in a major national agreement, the pattern becomes widespread. This happened in 1918-19 with the 47 or 48 hour week, again in 1946-47 with the 44 hour week and again in 1959-61 with the 42 hour week.

While lower working hours represent a major benefit to arise from growing rates of productivity, it is by no means the only or even the major benefit to accrue to employees. Employees, when bargaining, have been able to trade off higher wages for lower hours and to forgo one in order to have more of the other. Between 1850 and 1950, a third of the national increase in productivity was taken in the form of reduced working hours and two-thirds taken in the form of extra wages. Since 1950, the proportion of national productivity increase taken in the form of reduced hours has fallen to eight per cent and the bulk has gone to financing wage increases and the enormous growth in consumption of consumer durables over the last three decades.[78] A similar pattern has occurred in the USA where 75 or 80 per cent of the productivity dividend has gone to increasing wages rather than leisure.[79]

Trade unions, in advocating a further cut in the working week, suggest that since the rate of reduction of weekly hours has slowed up in the last 30 years, given currently rising levels of unemployment, the time is ripe for further reductions. Moreover, a 35 hour week has been part of official TUC policy since its adoption under the influence of Jack Jones in 1972. But a question must surround the general willingness of employees to trade-off further reductions in hours against pay increases. The strongest evidence for this is the remarkable consistency in the length of the working week in real terms since the end of the last war. In that period, the standard working week for full-time male manual workers has fallen from 46 to 40 hours, but the actual number of hours worked has remained about 46, overtime having increased from almost zero to about six hours per week. Clearly any future proposals to reduce the working week should be seen in this context and a fall in basic hours should not be merely compensated for by additional overtime working at enhanced rates. It is in this context that the adoption of shiftworking takes on significance and will be returned to again.

The debate on worksharing focusses on two main aspects – to what extent does it reduce unemployment in the short run and also its effects on employers' costs and therefore job stability in the long run.[80] The effect on employers' costs in reducing the standard working week has been based on the assumption that employees are seeking to cut hours without any reduction in previous basic pay. A recent review of the trade union position towards worksharing has concluded:

> There has never been any question that workers take any real cut in pay to work shorter hours. No loss of earnings is an essential precondition.[81]

In putting the argument for a cut in the working week as a means of reducing unemployment, Hughes[82] has suggested that since the 40 hour week applies mainly to manual workers (80 per cent of the total number), manual workers are the group most affected by unemployment (they account for 80 per cent of unemployment) and Britain is one of the few countries where a differential exists between the basic hours of manual and non-manual workers, so a cut in the working week to 37 or 35 hours would be a timely solution to unemployment. He reckons that a 35 hour week could reduce registered unemployment by half a million and suggests that the adoption of 35 hour working associated with a productivity bargain involving the adoption of shiftwork and overtime could mean that 30 to 40 per cent of the increased cost might be offset by increased efficiency.

A different view has been offered by researchers at the Department of Employment.[83] They argue that it is highly uncertain how many extra jobs would be created by a reduction of normal hours. On the basis of past experience, a fall in the working week led to an increase in overtime being worked. When the normal week was reduced from 44 to 40 hours almost half the potential for increasing jobs was lost through high levels of overtime. Additionally, a cut in the working week might lead to a higher output per man hour, such as was experienced during the three day week of 1974, which would again not greatly affect unemployment. Finally, output could fall and if additional workers with the appropriate skills were not available amongst the unemployed, the levels of unemployment would again not be affected. Because of these variables, the precise employment effect of a cut in the working week was difficult to predict, but the researchers concluded that a 35 hour week could reduce registered unemployment by anything from 100,000 to nearly 500,000, but if weekly earnings were maintained total labour costs would increase by between six to eight per cent. A smaller cut to 38 hours would increase labour costs by two to three per cent, but would have a substantially smaller effect on unemployment. The Department's estimate of a six to eight per cent increase in employers' unit labour costs to introduce a 35 hour week is similar to the TUC's estimate contained in their Economic Review of 1978, but well below the cost estimated by the Engineering Employers Federation who put the figure at 14 to 20 per cent without productivity improvements.[84]

The main problem associated with the shorter working week is that its precise effects on unemployment are uncertain. It could result in a fall in output, more overtime working or tighter manning levels and rises in productivity with little consequent effect on unemployment. Moreover, its possible impact on the unit labour costs of employers are inflationary and damaging to longer term employment prospects. Notwithstanding this critique, some estimates suggest that unemployment can be reduced by this approach and it is therefore likely to continue to feature in trade union bargaining claims.

Reductions in overtime

It has already been noted that overtime is extensively worked by manual workers in British industry and the logical implication of this for worksharing is that cuts in overtime could be translated into full-time jobs for the unemployed. The extent to which this is so will depend on the nature of the overtime worked. Many writers have suggested that much overtime working in British industry has become 'institutionalized' and little related to fluctuations in market demand,[85] with the result that cuts in overtime are likely to lead to higher productivity with little effect on unemployment. Where it is worked to meet seasonal peaks or carry out special tasks overtime may well be more cost effective than recruiting new employees, since it does not involve additions to the fixed costs of employment through such items as National Insurance contributions, pension contributions, holiday pay, sick pay, fringe benefits, hiring and training costs and other employment overheads. But where overtime levels are persistently high, a large cut in overtime is more likely to require the recruitment of new employees if past output levels are to be maintained.

Some illustrations of the possible impact of overtime cuts on unemployment have also come from the Department of Employment.[86] For example, such is the extent of overtime working in manufacturing industry that if all the overtime hours worked could be translated into full-time jobs, sufficient jobs would be created in the manufacturing sector alone to provide positions for all the one and a half million unemployed. This of course is purely theoretical, since many employers are using overtime for the very reasons of flexibility outlined above, but nevertheless a valid point is made. The same study also considered those groups working excessively long hours. If half the hours worked in excess of 48 by male manual workers could be translated into full-time jobs, the unemployment register could be reduced by over 100,000.

No one really knows how much overtime is institutionalized and how much economically necessary. In the same way, no one can be certain about the effect of reduced overtime on creating new jobs. Currently, trade union leaders are showing interest in cutting overtime as a means of worksharing to cut unemployment. The main problem is getting acceptance on the shop floor. In a recent article, it was noted that the Amalgamated Union of Engineering Workers had mounted a poster and leaflet campaign against overtime, but it was concluded:

The campaign was a miserable failure. District committees, where the real shop floor power lies, refused to respond. For most manual workers, overtime is a necessary fact of life, a custom and practice that not even the recession has managed to destroy.[87]

In a situation where over half the full-time manual workforce regularly works overtime (and the latter amounts to over 14 per cent of gross national earnings amongst such employees[88]) the problems of overtime reduction become clear. Add to this the fact that many of those working high levels of overtime also earn low basic wages and the problems are compounded. Nevertheless, many of the genuine productivity deals of the 1960s involved the substantial reduction or elimination of overtime[89] and could probably do so again, but the role of overtime reduction as a worksharing measure seems problematical.

Extension of shiftworking

Despite traditional trade union reservations about shiftworking because of its implications for health and domestic arrangements, some recent arguments emanating from trade union quarters see the extension of shiftworking, which currently involves about a quarter of all manual employees, as a cost effective way of cutting unemployment. Unlike a number of other approaches to worksharing, the extension of shiftworking has the potential for increasing employment while at the same time reducing unit costs through a fall in overheads resulting from a fuller use of plant and machinery but would be appropriate only where demand for a product is expanding fast. From a company's point of view, the adoption of shiftworking could be particularly advantageous where high levels of overtime are regularly worked. In terms of its effect on cost inflation, where market demand justifies it, the extension of shiftworking would seem to be a cost effective approach to worksharing which management and unions might both support.

Increased annual holidays

Although annual holiday entitlement has risen quite sharply in recent years, further extensions are suggested as part of a worksharing approach to unemployment. The majority of manual workers in Britain in 1965 were entitled to two weeks annual holiday; by 1970 half received between three and four weeks; and by 1975 half received between three and four weeks, and a further third four weeks or more.[90] Apart from worksharing arguments, it is also suggested that pressure to raise annual holiday entitlement in the UK may stem from domestic comparisons with Western Europe. The table below suggests that holiday entitlement in the UK lags behind the entitlement in most Western European countries.[91] In addition to this an EEC recommendation issued in 1975 states that all workers in Community countries should have progressed to four weeks annual holiday by the end of 1978, and further pressure is expected from the European TUC to make this five weeks by the end of 1980. But these are only recommendations and do not have the backing of law.

Country	Annual leave in days	Days of public holiday
Belgium	24	10
Denmark	24	$9\frac{1}{2}$
France	24–30	7–10
Germany	18–26	10–13
Ireland	15–18	7
Italy	24	17
Luxembourg	20–22	10
Netherlands	20–22	7
UK	15–20	7

Both annual entitlement and the number of public holidays in the UK are below those of most Western European countries, but the impact of increasing annual holiday entitlement as a worksharing measure to reduce unemployment must inevitably be small. Holiday leave can generally be covered by replanning work schedules and lost time can be absorbed by increased overtime working, temporary workers, and more flexible working arrangements. The research done by the Department of Employment suggests that if the working time lost by granting an extra week's holiday to all employees could be translated into full-time jobs, registered unemployment would be reduced by between 25,000 to over 100,000 and labour costs would rise by about two per cent.[92] Again, given the alternatives available to meet holiday contingencies, the impact of increased holidays on unemployment is likely to be minimal. Nevertheless, aspirations for greater leisure and comparisons with European practice are

76

likely to mean that additional holidays will feature in negotiations based on a worksharing approach.

Sharing of jobs

The past trends and future projections discussed in part II indicated that part-time working was on the increase. One further approach to worksharing, as yet not highly developed, is the concept of job sharing, which may be defined as 'a voluntary work arrangement in which two people hold responsibility for what was formerly one full-time position.'[93] The approach enables two people to share one job based on a firm agreement between the employer and employees concerned. It might be that the sharers divide morning and afternoon coverage between them, or alternate whole weeks, or indeed any other acceptable combination of hours. The approach might be particularly appropriate for older workers approaching retirement which, in addition to assisting the unemployment problem, would assist in lessening the individual problems of transition from work to retirement, on the lines of current Swedish practice. In addition, such an approach might be used in the training of successors. In the USA, jobsharing has been applied amongst teachers, social workers, secretaries, receptionists and clerical workers, and in the Netherlands by the grocery chain faced with recruitment problems. Currently in Britain Barclay's Bank employ 2,000 part-time employees on a job-sharing basis.[94]

A number of advantages are claimed for jobsharing, most notably that it gives greater flexibility to employees to combine work and non-work roles and may therefore act as a recruitment attraction where recruitment problems are being experienced. It is also claimed to reduce absenteeism because employees have free time in the day to do those things which might otherwise be done in work time (doctor, dentist, the visits of the gasman, the plumber and so on). Against the concept are the problems of communication between the jobsharers, which can be overcome, and the additional cost of employment overheads, at least those contained in statutes.

While jobsharing is of itself a possible new approach to alleviating some recruitment problems, it may not, as some believe, greatly reduce unemployment since it may merely attract new entrants into the labour market looking for part-time work.

77

While the approaches to worksharing discussed up to now have been concerned largely with attempting to reduce the hours spent at work in order to reduce unemployment, the last three measures to be discussed below have the accent on removing certain categories of people from the labour market itself. The approaches discussed above were largely the responsibility of employers to initiate, in some instances jointly with trade unions, but this last group additionally involves the role of the state: retirement ages and the time spent in full-time education. The role of the state does not preclude initiatives by organizations in these areas, but may impose parameters of constraint upon them and the distinction for this reason is worth making.

Early retirement

Early retirement has been suggested as one approach to work-sharing to enable young people to take up jobs vacated by those retiring. The current retirement age for men of 65 was first laid down in the Pension Act of 1928 and the age for women of 60 was first established in an Act of 1940. In the years following, life expectancies have increased considerably and legislation has been passed to promote equality of the sexes in respect of pay and opportunities, but retirement ages have remained unaltered. Retirement ages have therefore also been considered within the framework of worksharing.

Research has suggested that a reduction in the retirement age of men to 60 could reduce registered unemployment by up to 600,000. However, the cost associated with such a move would be heavy. Apart from the cost to the State of extra pension payments and reduced income tax and national insurance revenue, it has been estimated that the increased costs resulting from actuarial revisions to private occupational pension schemes would increase employers' labour costs by over four per cent for good schemes and by two per cent on average.[95] Such a reduction in retirement age could create further inflation as a result of increased public expenditure and increased unit labour costs for firms. Moreover, a five year reduction in retirement age for men might not have a 'pro rata' effect on the reduction of employment. Firms may not replace those who retire early, but use the opportunity to shed labour and raise productivity. Equally, the problem of skill shortage may be exacerbated since firms may be unable to find from amongst those offering themselves for work

78

the skills required.

On the face of it, there is evidence from Britain and elsewhere that retirement ages are falling already.[96] In January 1977 the Government introduced the Job Release Scheme which enabled employees within one year of statutory pension age to retire and make way for a registered unemployed person, a condition of the scheme. A total of nearly 48,000 people took advantage of the scheme in the first two years of its operation and the original scheme has since been extended, lowering the early retirement age to 62 for men (59 for women) and enhancing the weekly sum payable. Unions have generally shown interest in the Job Release concept. The North West TUC had, prior to the recent amendments, urged a reduction in the age of eligibility with higher levels of compensation and the General and Municipal Workers' Union had proposed grant-aided part-time working as people approached retirement.

Looking at early retirement practices amongst employers in the UK, research by the British Institute of Management (BIM) a few years ago suggested that at that time early retirement was comparatively rare.[97] Among the 424 companies surveyed, only nine per cent of retirements were early which may be contrasted with the wishes of individual managers surveyed, 80 per cent of whom would ideally like to have retired before age 65. Of the retirements which were early, the majority were forced on the individual through ill health or were at the company's request (frequently a redundancy situation). In only a small number of companies was early retirement based on the fulfilment of a length of service qualification, and in many cases this was not an absolute right but was granted only with company consent.

A more recent survey in the UK has concluded that lower retirement ages are found predominantly in the public sector, frequently 60 for men and 55 for women.[98] The Civil Service have in addition used early retirement to smooth out manpower planning problems. Senior Civil Servants have been offered tax free lump sum payments plus a full pension if they agree to retire at an earlier age than above to free promotion blockages. This became necessary because of the large proportion of top civil servants who were due to retire in the next few years and phased retirement would enable younger people to come through and gain experience. Elsewhere in the public sector early retirement has recently been introduced in the mining industry. Currently, underground workers who have 20 years service are able to

79

volunteer for retirement at 62, the age limit being phased down to 60 over the next two years. Entitlement includes a lump sum payment of £500 and two-thirds final wages until the age of 65. The National Coal Board (NCB) estimates that 93 per cent of those eligible (nearly 7,000 miners) will take advantage of the schemes at an estimated cost in the first year of £12 million. In the private sector, an Incomes Data Services (IDS) survey found that early retirement was rarer, although Lloyds Bank, ICI and Turner and Newell all had a lower retirement age for men; and several other companies, such as Philips and Little-woods, had a lower age limit for management only. The IDS report concluded that:

> many of the companies . . . seemed interested in lowering the retirement age for all employees . . . the main factor against it was the high cost involved if there was to be no financial detriment to the employee.[99]

Current evidence, while not extensive, would suggest that early retirement is not widespread in the UK but that it may be growing, particularly among executives and senior managers.

Further evidence may be cited from outside Britain. Early retirement is more frequent in the USA where the majority of pension schemes provide vested rights to early retirement, meaning that employees who meet certain age and service requirements can retire of their own volition, without the need for company consent and automatically receive a pension. In West Germany, all men and women can retire at 63 on a slightly reduced pension. Both France and Belgium have optional early retirement schemes from age 60 and in Italy, where the normal age for men is 60, options are available for retirement at 57, with the payment of allowances corresponding to retirement pensions.

Yet despite these developments there is no evidence to suggest that pressures for worksharing will accelerate these trends nor indeed is there any evidence that early retirement enjoys whole-sale support amongst employees. In Britain, the Union of Post Office Workers has demanded the option of being able to stay on to 65 in the event of early retirement proposals being imple-mented and in the USA the right to work to the age of 70 has recently been embodied in employment legislation. The likeli-hood in Britain is that the pressures will grow for early retirement options, rather than a statutorily reduced pension age, rights which only some employees will want to exercise but which will create additional problems for manpower planners within companies.

Extension of education

There are two ways in which the extension of education can make a contribution to worksharing. First, it can raise the age at which young people leave the full-time education system and enter the world of work. Secondly, periods of educational leave may also increasingly become a feature of working life.

To look at the first of these developments, the implication is not that the minimum school leaving age is likely to be raised further because this is unlikely of itself to serve any useful purpose. But the previous part suggested that more young people are voluntarily embarking on sixth-form courses and increasing numbers are entering higher education. This will automatically have the effect of delaying their age of entry into full-time employment. At the same time, the current expansion of work experience and vocational training programmes, run under the auspices of the MSC and designed to bridge the gap between school and work, suggests that effectively many more young people will be extending the time spent in some form of full-time education or training and that ultimately many of them will not enter formal employment until the age of 18 or 19. This is evidenced in the words of a recent consultative paper on education and training for the 16 to 18 year olds which stated that attempts were being made 'to establish a universal scheme of education and training opportunities for all this age group'.[100]

But extended education should not be seen as applicable only to young people. The more swiftly technology changes, the more swiftly skills and knowledge become obsolete, and for increasing numbers of people education and training are likely to become recurrent processes in order to meet the new demands posed by technical and social change. Thus, extended education or educational leave can meet company training objectives and contribute towards worksharing. Moreover, whether related to our work needs or not, the concept of sabbatical leave is growing in importance and has already featured as part of trade union claims in major national negotiations. Some companies also have developed the idea of sabbaticals, for so long the preserve of the academic, and have frequently related it to some wider social or community activity to be undertaken by individuals. There is of course the possibility that sabbatical leave unrelated to some specific study or social project may result in employees 'moonlighting' by taking on another job during the sabbatical, but that is a matter for judgement in the light of individual circumstances.

As discussions elsewhere in this book have indicated, training and education are increasingly playing a more important role in peoples' lives and it is therefore not surprising that many are turning towards them as a positive approach to the problem of unemployment.

Worksharing policies in Europe: the approach of the EEC

Having summarized the various approaches in the UK, it is worth briefly considering developments in Europe. Unemployment in the EEC at present totals six million (5.7 per cent of the work force), of which two million are estimated to be young people, a rise of 400 per cent in the last eight years. As in Britain, demographic forecasts for the EEC show that the number of people of working age will increase by about one million per year between now and the mid 1980s, a significant proportion of which will be young people. This in addition to a period of reduced growth (which averaged two per cent between 1974 and 1977 compared with four per cent between 1970 and 1973) emphasizes the deteriorating employment prospects throughout the Community as a whole during the next decade.

Significant discussion of unemployment at the EEC level dates from early 1976 when the Economic and Social Committee urged governments to work out national targets for reductions in unemployment levels. In June 1977 the Commission recommended the adoption by Member States of vocational training and work experience programmes aimed at young people under 25 and member states were asked to report back on the measures taken to implement the recommendation by the end of 1978. Also in June 1977, the Tripartite Conference of social partners announced a joint study programme to be carried out through the Standing Employment Committee and the Economic Policy Committee which would include the study of the cost effectiveness and implications for industrial performance of different means

82

of worksharing. The studies proposed by the Tripartite Conference would form the basis of proposals for action within the Community.

The document on worksharing was subsequently produced and having considered a wide range of worksharing measures, selected the following areas for possible action at community level:

Overtime working: the possible introduction of some instrument designed to discourage overtime working

Restrictions on shift working: although not precise, guidelines for reform would be forthcoming, particularly in relation to night work

Extension of the right to training: rather than raising the school leaving age, consideration would be given to provisions to develop training for young people during the transition between school and working life.[101]

The Commission did not feel that it wanted to intervene in matters such as the length of the working week or paid holidays since practices varied from one country to another, beyond reiterating their 1976 recommendation for a 40 hour week and four weeks paid holiday in all member states. They did however feel that there were areas which were worthy of further attention in relation to worksharing. These included:

the role of the Social Security system on more flexible employment measures

flexible or lower retirement ages

the role of temporary work and associated agencies and their effect on worksharing objectives

the role of part-time work and its relationship to social legislation, employee relations and sex discrimination.

Few firm proposals have yet emerged from this, with the exception that restrictions on night shiftwork, which anyway ran counter to most views of worksharing in the UK, have been dropped while programmes to alleviate the problems of youth unemployment have been further developed. But clearly the Commission have a co-ordinating role to play if worksharing proposals are going to be carried any further amongst member states in order to ensure that no individual nation loses its competitive advantage by adopting worksharing in isolation.

Worksharing and Trade Unions: some trends in Europe

The role of the Brussels-based European Trade Union Confederation (ETUC) seems to have been influential in EEC
thinking as regards worksharing. Significant pressure to further
examine worksharing has emanated from the ETUC, particularly
following their adoption of a shorter working week policy under
the influence of Jack Jones at their London Conference in 1976.
The ETUC has since urged action at an EEC level particularly
in relation to the 35 hour week, retirement at 60 and the extension
of annual holiday entitlement to a total of six weeks. They have
also gained support within the Commission on other worksharing
initiatives mentioned above, particularly the reduction of overtime, shiftworking and the development of training programmes
bridging the transition between school and work. At the same
time the ETUC has been urging national union federations to
pursue worksharing strategies and this may be reflected in recent
trends in collective bargaining in Europe.

In the forefront of developments have been the unions in
Belgium where, following a wave of strikes in the spring of 1978
in the public sector, the government conceded a 38 hour week
against a previous 40 hours to employees in that sector, with the
unions demanding a further cut to 36 hours by 1980. These
concessions in the public sector have already had important
effects on private sector negotiations, with a 38 hour week having
been conceded in the docks, printing, chemicals, oil refining and
engineering industries. In West Germany, unions are seeking
longer holidays and discussions have commenced on reduced
weekly hours, flexible hours and the removal of overtime. In
particular, the printing union IG Druck, the food and catering
union NGG, and IG Metall are pursuing a 35 hour week. In
Sweden the annual holiday entitlement has been raised from four
to five weeks excluding public holidays. Recently in France a
budget package included tax measures to discourage overtime.
But the unions, particularly the CGT, have demanded further
measures including a reduction of the working week from 40 to
35 hours without loss of pay. All these measures are in addition
to the developments in early retirement discussed above.

The review of trends in Europe indicates that not only are
worksharing solutions to unemployment being increasingly urged

by trade unions, but also that measures to reduce the labour supply will increasingly be considered by all governments in Western Europe.[102]

Worksharing and trade unions in Britain

The issue of unemployment has clearly been of major importance to the trade union movement and recommendations for its amelioration have featured widely both in the statements of the TUC and individual unions.

The TUC's Annual Report for 1977 noted that 'unemployment and inflation have been issues of major concern to the General Council'[103] and a motion was carried which expressed the 'deepest concern at the continued intolerably high level of unemployment in the UK with a continuing erosion of job opportunities'.[104] In terms of policy measures, the *Annual Report* and the 1978 TUC *Economic Review*, urged the Government:

to adopt a reflationary economic strategy
to continue subsidies aimed at relieving youth unemployment
to embark on a massive expansion of training and education schemes, work experience and work preparation programmes, and opportunities for 16 plus and higher education
to substantially expand the public sector programme
to give priority to the 35 hour working week without loss of pay and reduce overtime working where it is being used as an alternative to employing extra staff.

A further motion was adopted at the 1977 Annual Congress which urged further study of the changing pattern of employment to include working days, the length of the working week, holidays, retirement ages and the need for cultural and recreational activities to be developed.[105] Clearly, then, the TUC is heavily committed to many of the approaches to worksharing previously discussed as a means of combating higher levels of unemployment.

Many individual unions have also been putting their weight behind some forms of worksharing. Most notable have been the calls for a reduction in the working week, usually to 35 hours, which during the last bargaining round was actively pursued by all the nation's largest unions. Actual concessions of shorter working weeks have been few in number. Last year after nine months of action, the Post Office Engineering Union secured a

85

$37\frac{1}{2}$ hour week, although this action was in pursuit of a parity claim rather than worksharing. Elsewhere, miners are working a $37\frac{1}{2}$ hour week, nurses are progressing to $37\frac{1}{2}$ hours by 1981 and firemen also are progressively moving to shorter hours. Action in other areas of worksharing has been slight, although some unions have expressed interest in the extension of shiftwork, sabbaticals are being included in some collective bargaining claims (for example by the Transport and General Workers in the Ford claim) and early retirement has been secured for faceworkers by the Miners' Union.

It cannot be doubted that there is general concern among trade unions about unemployment. Nor can it be doubted that some of the worksharing measures discussed here will increasingly feature in trade union demands. Yet one must be sceptical of the support for some of these measures by the rank and file of trade unions and the mechanics involved in translating cuts in working time into new jobs, especially in a period of low growth.

Worksharing and organizations

The initial question for organizations examining worksharing is cost. As pointed out above, there is general agreement from various perspectives that some aspects of worksharing represent a cost to organizations, although opinions differ, not surprisingly, on how much the cost would be. It was also suggested that some measures, such as the reduction of overtime, may meet with the local opposition of trade unions. Nevertheless, discussions within trade unions, the EEC, and developments both in Britain and Western Europe suggest that a number of the worksharing measures discussed in this section are likely to remain issues for debate as long as unemployment remains high.

Clearly, where the adoption of worksharing measures is likely to have a substantial effect on unit labour costs, they cannot serve the long-term interests of employment expansion. But a number of these measures need not have such an effect and are worthy of closer examination. Early retirement, provided that it is not imposed compulsorily, while representing an additional cost to the organization might nevertheless hold benefits that outweigh these costs. Evidence discussed earlier suggested that a large number of older employees would like to retire earlier than 65. But further questions need to be asked. For example, what impact would this have on the effectiveness of the organization? What effect also does promotion blockage have on younger managers? Considering manual workers, how would the productivity of the older worker compare with a younger one? This is not to advocate the wholesale adoption of early retirement, far from it. On the other side of the coin, it is necessary to consider the loss of knowledge, skill and experience to organizations of older employees. These are matters which we should have already given attention in our manpower plan. Where this has not been so, the issue of early retirement will need very careful consideration.

The reduction of overtime, possibly associated with the adoption of shiftwork within the framework of a productivity deal, might be another useful approach. Jobsharing may be preferred by an increasing number of employees. How many of our existing employees, for example, might prefer to work in such a way and what are the potential costs as well as benefits to the organization? Finally, there is the role of extended education. Both the expansion of vocationally-orientated education to improve the transition from school to work and later periods of study-leave related to training or retraining in occupational skills could both assist in the solution of national manpower problems (by reducing skill shortage and raising productivity) and assist in alleviating some of the effects of unemployment.

Worksharing requires careful but critical examination and where unit costs are likely to be forced upwards without any measurable benefit to the organization, it is likely to be harmful to longer term employment prospects. In the future, as in the past, shorter working time will in the last analysis be facilitated by a substantial growth in productivity as a result of investment in new technology and the adoption of improved working methods. Yet we should also remember that the level of demand in the home market for our organizations' goods and services is dependent on the indigenous population purchasing them. If increasing numbers of that population are without jobs then they are also without the income to buy the goods or services we are offering. With falling demand, our costs will rise and productivity will fall and in this lies the dilemma for organizations.

8

Technological change and organizations

Reference was made earlier to an expected increase in the pace of technological change in the next few years and this chapter aims to look at the implications of this for organizations.

It is important to note that technology (ie the machines or equipment and the way they are laid out) within the workplace, be it office or factory, is not merely something to be manipulated by the workforce, but it significantly affects the relationship between the individual, his job and those around him. Let us look at an example. At one time, many of the goods which we bought were hand-made by craftsmen in small workshops. The work they did was highly skilled requiring a number of years training, the craftsman was totally responsible for the quality of the final product and the workshop provided an informal atmosphere where the workpeople could discuss, communicate with each other or otherwise interact socially whenever they wished. Technical change, the growth of the size of industrial organizations and specialization arising out of an increased division of labour have changed this substantially. The chances are that the same goods today are produced on production lines, in large factories, using automated machinery, manned by relatively unskilled operatives. These kinds of changes appear to have taken place over a long time-span covering many generations, yet at the same time specific changes in production systems with new work methods are continually being introduced in a relatively short space of time and as the pace of technological change quickens, so this time-span becomes shorter.

The above account serves to illustrate in a stark way how

technology can affect the skills required at work and the way we interact with others, and it is for these reasons that much research evidence has offered the view that technology has an important effect on the behaviour of people within organizations.

There is evidence to support the view that assembly line technology can lead to negative attitudes towards work for a number of reasons. Social interaction, which has been viewed as an important element in motivation, is prevented by the noise and the demands or layout of the production line.[106] 'Alienation' has been said to occur also because of the structure of the jobs themselves: particularly the lack of scope to control the pace of work, both the quality and the working method and a failure to see or understand how the job fits into the overall process or finished product.[107] Other types of technology on the other hand, produce different attitudes and lower levels of alienation. Craft technology, for example, permits the kinds of control over the task and scope for social interaction said to be lacking in mass production technology. So also does the newly developing and highly automated process-production technology, such as is found in the petroleum, chemical, steel and increasingly in the food and drink industries. Within such a technology, the machine operator becomes a process controller, working in a pleasant environment at automated control panels and exercising more control over and responsibility over the production process than under mass production systems. This kind of technical system is seen as one way in which technology might develop in the future.[108]

It should not however be assumed that any particular type of technology is immutable and will inevitably produce certain kinds of attitudes and motivation. Much work done by the Tavistock Institute on job redesign suggests that management has more flexibility than is generally believed in adapting technical systems, particularly repetitive production-line work, to social needs. One illustrative example may be quoted from the coal-mining industry.[109] Prior to highly mechanized working, faceworkers had worked in informal groups, usually groups of friends who had chosen to work with each other, allocated the various tasks in a day's work amongst themselves and shared the bonus earnings of the group amongst its members. Following the introduction of mechanized working and mass production methods, the old informal working groups were disbanded, each person was allocated a specific task to perform and a working team in which to perform it. Despite the introduction of mechanized working, the gains expected in productivity did not materialize. The Tavistock team suggested that although new mechanized technology had been introduced and placed certain limitations on the social arrangements of the workplace, the extensive break up of old working groups and the introduction of such extensive division of labour had not been *dictated* by the new technology. It was found in fact that most of the informal traditional working arrangements which had been popular with the men prior to mechanization could be reintroduced within the new technical environment and, having made these alterations, increased productivity could be achieved.

Technology has also been held to be an important influence on industrial relations.[110] In most organizations, certain departments or sections tend to incur more industrial unrest, while others tend to be trouble-free. This has also been related to the technology which may divide the workforce into key, highly integrated work groups who then have the power to hold up the whole production process in pursuit of their own sectional interests. Such a process can lead to competitive bargaining between different work groups and thus challenge the authority of management, unions themselves and the formal collective bargaining process in maintaining orderly industrial relations.

Finally, reference should be made to the role of technology in shaping organization structure. Woodward has indicated that the most effective organization structure (for example, the length of lines of command or span of control of each manager) should not be derived from some universal principles of efficient administration but must be related to the technology within which the organization operates.[111] Taking three major types of technological systems – unit or small batch, mass production and process production – it was demonstrated that the most successful firms within each of these production systems were those which were able to adapt organization structure to the demands of different technical systems. Although it is beyond the scope of this book to go into the specific organizational adaptations prescribed, they included such issues as the length of lines of command and number of levels in the management hierarchy, the span of control of the Chief Executive, the number of functional management specialists, the number of persons controlled by supervisors and the ratios of indirect labour to direct.

One further influence of technology on organization should also be mentioned. Work by Burns and Stalker suggests that the pace of technological change and innovation in the product market in which the firm is operating is also relevant to organization structure.[112] Some industries, such as the electronics industry, face a market in which success or failure depends largely on innovation and the ability to be first in the market with a technically superior product. As a result, permanent and dynamic change outside the firm requires a similarly adaptive internal organization structure. This Burns and Stalker refer to as an 'organic' structure, which is an informal multi-disciplinary task-orientated structure of working groups, sufficiently flexible to meet the dynamics of change and the need to innovate in order to survive in such a product market. Other industries face a particularly stable market environment since the nature of the product and the demand for it change little, resulting in fewer pressures to adapt the organization's structure. In such a situation, a 'mechanistic' or bureaucratic hierarchy with little flexibility may be sufficient to meet the firm's needs. Given the increasing pace of technological change and the competition to sell high-quality goods at an economic price, it would appear that the 'organic' form is becoming an increasingly appropriate structure for organizations.

Although technology is by no means the only factor in understanding organizations, this brief review suggests that it is nevertheless an important one. Bearing in mind the implications of technical change outlined here, we need to consider the impact of new developments in technology, particularly computer technology and the microprocessor, on organizations.

The organizational impact of microelectronic technology

In chapter 4 it was concluded that while a wide range of applications of microprocessors could be envisaged resulting in new products and the technical improvement of existing ones, the major impact was likely to be on industrial and manufacturing processes and office systems and procedures. What follows is not intended as a comprehensive analysis of possible applications of microprocessors, which in any case is the subject of current research, but those interested in pursuing the topic further may wish to refer to the growing number of references available.[113]

Mass and batch production: Microprocessor control can be applied to any mass production machinery currently controlled electro-mechanically. Car manufacturers outside the UK are introducing microprocessor control to some aspects of production, currently paint-spraying and welding, although applications in this area could foreseeably be extended. Plants for packaging, bottling, food processing, paper or glass making, textile machinery, and industrial sewing machines are also amongst some of their potentially wide reaching applications. In some instances, micro-electronics provide the opportunity to automate totally the manufacturing process. Japan currently has 70,000 computerized robots in industry, about one-third of these being in the car industry and the Japanese are currently planning a complete machine tool factory run entirely by robots and computers. At Fiat in Italy, a production line is operated by 20 robots welding parts of a car together. In the USA there are a range of robot research projects which keep a low profile for fear of attracting union hostility. Particularly appropriate applications of robots seem to be to monotonous or hazardous work and although robots are not currently highly sophisticated and are relatively expensive, there will inevitably be technical improvement and cost reductions within the next few years.

Process production: this would include the batch processing control of bulk solids or liquids as in the refining, chemical or brewing industries, where microprocessor-based equipment could be responsible for the operation of a complete plant, including the diagnosis and rectification of faults or irregularities.

Warehousing: the handling of materials, particularly through the use of the fork lift truck, is already an area where automation has made an impact. The automated warehouse has been a sector of high growth in the USA, Germany and Japan and although much slower to grow in Britain, a small number of fully automated warehouses have been in existence since the early 1970s. Regarding future developments, two recent analysts have concluded that in relation to the retail distribution industry:

> it is highly likely that the next generation of warehouses built for such customers will be of the fully automated type.[114]

Office administration: the earlier discussion on changing occupational structure indicated that employment in administrative, secretarial and clerical occupations has been one of enormous expansion across the economy. This has also meant a substantial increase in costs for organizations and has led to closer examination of ways to control costs in this area. Traditionally, rationalization and automation have been used to raise productivity and reduce costs in a factory environment, but increasingly similar criteria, involving new technology, have been applied to the office. An important new piece of equipment is the 'word processor' which is basically an electric typewriter connected to a computer producing tapes (but with a window screen showing the last words typed). These tapes are then fed into a Visual Display Unit (VDU). A number of advantages of the equipment may be noted. The average secretary spends a high proportion of her time correcting errors, retyping drafts, or typing standard letters or forms. Using the original computer tape, pages of type can be recalled to the VDU, the letters, sentences, or paragraphs altered, keyed in and the word processor will instantly produce a revised document. This document can be kept on tape for later reference or recall and may be reprinted whenever required. Use of a word processor also means that all filing can be kept in a computer memory bank rather than as physical pieces of paper filling countless drawers and cabinets. Future developments in this field could include the direct linking of word processing machines between the offices of different organizations providing instant communication and reply. A more distant development, perhaps at the end of the decade, is the word processor which will comprehend the human voice and be able to type instantly and automatically any letter dictated to it. To return to the realms of current word processing technology, the human operator is still very much required, but the productivity of a secretary has been claimed to have increased by up to 100 per cent or more using a word processor with a net saving on cost spread over the life of the equipment. The implications of these developments not only relate to filing. The advent of cheap micro-computers will mean that many more forms of data collection and dissemination will become computer-based. The obvious implication for personnel managers is the computerization of personnel records in those organizations which have not so far felt it to be a viable proposition.

Telecommunications: the advent of instant written communication means that the Post Office will be in the centre of a computer-based communications revolution and currently plan to open the first computer-controlled 'System X' exchange in 1981 with the objective of a national system by 1990. This development is connected with the emergence of computerized communication mentioned above. It is reckoned that during the 1980s the use of conventional mail will decline and electronic mail will increase involving the passing of written texts through the telephone system, based on a growing number of teletext receivers in both offices and private homes.

Retail distribution: in addition to the growth of automated warehousing in the retail distribution industry referred to earlier, new check-out terminals incorporating microprocessors are being introduced, capable of adding bills, instantly debiting the cost to the client's bank account and at the same time measuring stock movements for the purposes of control or re-ordering.

These are just some of the implications of microprocessors for organizations and it is unlikely that many readers will have failed to recognize where their organizations fit into this picture. It is now worth turning attention to the benefits and the problems associated with this new technology.

First, let us consider the benefits. These are quite simple: the falling cost of computer technology and the rising cost of wages and employment overheads indicates that a point is reached where the former is more cost effective. In addition, the new technology raises labour productivity, sometimes quite significantly. Let us look at some examples. Reference has already been made to the effect of word processors on cost reduction and an increase in labour productivity. In the manufacturing sector also, the effects of the introduction of microprocessor technology can be dramatic. In the USA, National Cash Register have incorporated microprocessors into cash registers and discarded almost all moving parts. This has done away with the need for the labour intensive activities of assembling mechanized parts and has contributed to a reduction of its manufacturing workforce by more than 50 per cent between 1970 and 1975.[115] Western Electric, who produce most of America's telephone equipment, have been able to cut back labour by 75 per cent between 1970 and 1976 in fault-finding, maintenance, repair and

94

installation work and by 50 per cent in manufacturing as a result of the introduction of microelectronics.[116] Apart from higher productivity and lower costs, it is suggested that microprocessors can reduce the need for dull, routine jobs and the necessity to work in a hazardous environment. In all, it is a technology which British industry must adopt if its products are to compete in world markets and a view is held amongst many people that Britain must *swiftly* apply this new technology if its industry is to survive. The Department of Industry have offered the view that microelectronics 'is not far behind the wheel in terms of industrial and commercial significance' and the Government's Advisory Council for Applied Research and Development have said of the technology that 'if we neglect or reject it as a nation, the United Kingdom will join the ranks of the underdeveloped countries.'[117] At the same time, the adoption of the technology will lead to substantial rises in productivity, income and the standard of living of the nation as a whole.

The main problems associated with the new technology are the social consequences arising from it, including displacement of labour and widespread redundancy of old skills. These problems are not in themselves insurmountable through the use of effective manpower and training policies. On the other hand, there is an influential school of thought which believes that this technology, *unlike* any previous technology, is the one which will substantially reduce employer's demand for labour. In other words, automation is reaching the point where people are no longer being required and this new technology, emerging alongside the growth in the labour force and slowing of the rate of economic growth described earlier, lends further support to the view that unemployment will soar upwards in the 1980s.

It is impossible to be dogmatic about the employment effects of microprocessor technology. New products and services may be generated. Current constraints on the growth of public services, for example the hospital service, education or social services may be relaxed if, in the economy as a whole, sufficient wealth is generated to pay for such expansion. But it is difficult to avoid the conclusion, given all the pressures in the labour market, that sufficient jobs are unlikely to be generated to reduce or even arrest some upward movement in unemployment.

Before leaving the question of the new technology of microelectronics for the moment, some perspective is necessary on the time-scale of its adoption. Despite the urgency in the Department of Industry's recent programme of national education on micro-processors, evidence points to the view that change will be gradual rather than swift. Research at the Science Policy Research Unit into the decision-making processes of manage-ment behind technical change suggests that much caution is exercised and there is a slow period of becoming familiar with the new technology before its application to the organization for which they are responsible.[118] This is not to deny the urgent need to apply the new technology. It is simply that its early application is probably more likely in small growing firms rather than in larger firms where the effect of substantial technological change on investment, organizational manpower and industrial relations require a longer gestation period.

To conclude, the next few years are likely to see substantial technical change with important effects on skills, training, re-training, job security, manpower planning, industrial relations and it is to this theme we shall return in the last part.

New technology and its impact on management

Management is largely concerned with receiving information, making decisions based on this information and taking the appropriate action. The development of 'information technology', as the emerging combination of computer and telecommunica-tions technology has been termed, means that more information can be provided to assist decision-making, more cheaply, more quickly and more reliably than under many current systems.

The significant effects of this will be to reduce the number of clerical, technical and junior managerial staff involved in providing this information, while at the same time it will provide more detailed and accurate control data. This is likely to improve the quality of managerial decision-making and may even indicate the optimum decision to be taken in a particular situation. This may, but not necessarily, have the effect of reducing the job satisfaction of managers. The new technology is likely to remove many of the more routine aspects of his job, leaving him to concentrate on two major tasks: solving those problems which require his skill and judgement based on the fullest possible information and paying more attention to man management, necessitated because those whom he manages are likely to be increasingly small in number but generally better qualified and working within an environment of rapidly increas-

96

ing change and innovation. Information technology is also likely to shorten the chain of command within organizations leading to a flatter, less hierarchical structure providing the possibility for improved internal communications.[119]

Three problem areas may emerge as a result of the impact of this new technology on management. The first concerns changes in management style, the second changes in inter-management relationships and the third changes in managerial careers.

First, looking at management style, a number of factors in the technical environment suggest that a participative rather than authoritarian style is becoming more appropriate. Information technology is making organizations less hierarchical or 'bureaucratic', there will be fewer levels in the chain of command and work groups will tend to be smaller and more skilled. These changes heighten both the practicality of and desire for participation. The increasing technical complexity of the market and its demands on internal flexibility, referred to in the discussion on organic organization structures[120], demonstrate its necessity. The tendency may therefore be to approach problems through some form of matrix organization or project teams built up of a number of different functional specialists brought together for a particular task. In such teams, the traditional authority attached to certain positions in the organization will be of less importance and the team leader is likely to be the person with the most appropriate skills given the particular problem being faced. Such teams would not necessarily be permanent but might well be disbanded on completion of a task. Project teams which aim to tap all the resources of organizations irrespective of hierarchical position by implication involve a participative approach to decision-making.[121]

The second area of change identified was in inter-management relationships, particularly the often debated but frequently applied classical distinction between 'line' and 'staff' managers, in which the former hold prime responsibility for achieving organizational goals and the latter (which in theory at least includes the personnel function) provide specialist advice to those taking line decisions. The concept has already been subjected to criticism by analysts of management practice, who have noted that much staff advice, for example the advice of the personnel department on observing disputes procedures or legislative requirements, effectively become executive commands.[122] But it is also suggested that the distinction becomes more problematic within the framework of technological change. Matrix management further blurs distinctions and information technology may make the 'advice' of staff departments increasingly mandatory. Finally, if line managers are to increase departmental responsibility for man management, the role of the personnel function is likely to become a more truly 'advisory' one. Clearly there are conflicts here which will require attention by organizations in the light of circumstances.

Thirdly, reference should be made to the possible effects of increasing technical complexity on management careers. Because the increasing pace of technological change is bringing about the swift obsolescence of technical skills, it has been suggested that 'for the first time in our history obsolescence seems to be an imminent problem for management because for the first time, the relevant advantage of experience over knowledge seems to be rapidly decreasing.'[123] The suggestion is that because recently acquired knowledge has become more vital to job success in an environment of change that this has come to outweigh the importance of years of experience. The result of this is that managers are tending to accelerate through the organization at a younger age and are reaching a career peak correspondingly younger. The effects are twofold. First, where organizations fail to accommodate to this process, young managers tend to 'job-hop' because of the blockage in promotion opportunities. Secondly, where organizations do accommodate to it, they are left with the problem of what to do with redundant executives in their mid 40s. For the future, careers may tend to develop downwards or laterally or require programmes of education and training to develop alternative new skills. Clearly, this latter problem may not affect all managers, depending on the type of organization, but it is currently a problem for some organizations and is likely to grow. The willingness to innovate and accept change has long been considered a major part of the role of management, but with employment security and the traditional management career threatened, attention to this problem is all the more urgent if technological innovation and change are to continue as driving forces within organizations.

Trade unions and technological change

The view has been expressed that 'automation . . . has brought the most difficult of bargaining issues – the clash of productivity and job protection – into the forefront of most negotiations.'[124] From the perspective of trade unions, technological change poses a difficult dilemma. On the one hand, trade unionists may appreciate the necessity for technological innovation to maintain long term job prospects, while in the short term they are concerned to protect the jobs of their members which may be threatened by proposed changes. The reaction of the Luddites (the hand-loom weavers and other textile workers who broke machines during the early days of the Industrial Revolution) is well known, but active opposition to technical innovation cannot be said to have formed a significant strategy of trade unionists since that time. Even as long ago as the late nineteenth century, the Webbs' analysis of trade union behaviour indicated that opposition to new machinery formed no major part of trade union tactics.[125] On the face of it, recent history suggests that much technological change has occurred against a background of trade union acceptance. Trade union cooperation in securing technical innovation and change, including in some cases a run-down in manpower, has been achieved in industries with widely ranging industrial relations climates – electronics, chemicals, oil-refining, steel, motor cars, shipbuilding and coal. But such a view understates the long and difficult negotiations which are likely to have preceded this negotiated acceptance of change and also overlooks major disputes which have arisen from this issue. The printing industry is a prime example of this. Our aim here will therefore be to consider what underlines trade union resistance to change before returning to the bargaining problems later.

Trade union strategy towards technological change is traditionally a defensive one and has frequently been the rationale behind protective mechanisms or 'restrictive practices'. New machinery, new working methods, virtually any form of technical change, means a change from the familiar to the unfamiliar and is treated with suspicion, sometimes justifiably and sometimes not so. At one extreme trade unions could seek to totally oppose technological change, changes in manning levels, changes in existing lines of demarcation or indeed any other aspect of traditional working practices which are threatened by change. But, as Mortimer has pointed out, in reality trade unions try to balance the need to preserve jobs with the possible benefits of change:

The real task for trade unionists is to cooperate in these

99

changes whilst at the same time ensuring through collective bargaining and by other industrial, economic and political means that those who are affected by change are protected and the benefits of change are widely distributed.[126]

Change is viewed as a matter for bargaining and some of the major concerns of trade unions facing technological change are likely to be as follows:

redundancy or the prospect of reduced job security in the future

loss of earnings by the change or removal of bonus or incentive schemes

the feeling that benefits are not being spread equally but that some groups are deriving greater benefit than others

distortion of internal relativities or differentials

flexible working practices leading to 'dilution' of skills, thereby threatening the existence of the craft itself

obsolescence of old skills

new skill requirements for which many people may be ill equipped

reduced promotion opportunities

increased pace of work

increased boredom and monotony

increased hazards

changed hours of work (unsocial hours, night work or shift work).

The bargaining objectives of trade unions will be twofold. First, to minimize the impact or disruption to the existing workforce by maintaining former manning levels, effort levels and skill mixes; seeking guarantees against redundancy and retraining, where necessary, of existing employees, supported by bans on external recruitment. Secondly, unions will aim to maximize the benefits of the new technology and higher productivity through substantial improvements in wages, hours, holidays and working conditions.

Trade unions want increasingly to make new technology a bargaining issue and in relation to, for example, new micro-electronic technology, are looking for early discussions on it with management in order to avoid 'Luddite' reactions later on. Trade unions generally accept and welcome the new technology but will argue that it cannot be at the expense of their members. As

Jenkins and Sherman have recently remarked in connection with the growth of computerization, 'unions cannot stand in the way of technological progress, but nor can they stand by and watch their members being sacrificed in its name.'[127] Clearly, when unemployment is high, this acts as a barrier to technological progress because workpeople are motivated to maintain the status quo and preserve jobs rather than accept technological change and risk unemployment. Particularly in the light of our earlier discussion that unemployment is likely to remain at existing levels or even increase further, the pressures against the acceptance of new technology are likely to increase. Currently within the trade union movement there is a good deal of concern over the effects of micro-electronic technology, which has led to calls for a Royal Commission of enquiry and even legislation to prevent companies adopting the new technology without prior trade union agreement, associated with which would be other changes such as those described in the chapter on 'work-sharing'.[128] The 1978 TUC Congress unanimously called for the formulation of policy on the social and industrial consequences of automation which would be later reported in the form of a draft policy statement. At the same time, Congress carried motions calling for worksharing – reduced working week, reduced state retirement age, longer holidays (including more public holidays and sabbaticals) and extended job creation and vocational training provisions.

Union policy, then, at least at national level, is not opposed outright to new technology but, as it has in the past, will be concerned with bargaining for the benefits resulting from increased productivity, while at the same time placing more emphasis than may have been the case in the past on measures to preserve jobs or stimulate further recruitment. Such pressures of course reduce the potential benefits of productivity gain which is a major reason why management may need to pursue a new approach to the planning and implementation of technical change, a theme to which we return in part IV.

One final point on the role of trade unions and the new technology may be made. Although there has been emphasis on the defensive approach of trade unions in the face of technical change, it should also be remembered that technical change tends to bring greater interdependence both between departments within an organization and between organizations in the society as a whole, and this can enhance the bargaining power of particular work-groups. Recently in this connection Jenkins and Sherman described data processing departments as 'high profile in industrial relations terms, that is to say that disruption of their normal functions deeply and speedily affect management of departments outside data processing.'[129] Public sector unions have used this tactic amongst government computer staff when pressing general pay claims, but this concentration of bargaining power should not be seen as a feature of computers alone, but rather as applicable wherever organizations invest in highly automated plant with a high ratio of capital to labour. Trade union members are, therefore, not all affected in the same way by new technology but the issue of job preservation is likely to remain the contentious one.

9

The impact of the legal framework

The growing role of the state and the use of legislation in the field of employment after the long tradition of 'voluntarism' were mentioned in the first chapter. The view was taken that intervention resulted primarily from economic difficulty and the influential diagnosis that manpower utilization and the industrial relations system were primarily at fault, rather than from any other major motivation for government intervention. The aim of legislation was to change current practice in order to rectify perceived shortcomings in either manpower utilization or industrial relations. This chapter aims to look at the impact of recent labour legislation or organizations and particularly to highlight how its impact is undergoing a change of emphasis.

Labour laws under full employment

Before looking at new developments, we must again pick up the theme that economic conditions played an influential role in shaping the legislation which has been enacted. Legislation in the fields of training and redundancy emphasized the importance of people as a valuable but scarce resource. This in turn served to highlight the role of the personnel function in advising on the utilization and development of this scarce resource. One of the major effects of industrial training legislation was to increase markedly the number of full-time training officers employed by companies[130] and, according to the CBI, its overall effect on organizations was 'to transform the whole climate of opinion and concentrate far more informed attention on training in British industry'.[131] Similarly, surveys of the impact of the redundancy payments legislation suggest that the increased costs of redundancy led to greater planning of manpower requirements within organizations.[132] Indeed, as Bell has pointed out, these Acts together with the growth of incomes policy with its focus on productivity, concentrated managements' attention on manpower utilization, which in turn stimulated company activity in the field of manpower planning.[133] As regards the impact of legislation on collective bargaining, it tended to bring more organizational issues into the realms of joint management–union regulation and reduced the area of unilateral management decision-making. The redundancy payment legislation is an example of this and led to an increased formalization of redundancy policies within collective agreements. Prior to the Act, very few companies considered the issue of redundancy or made redundancy payments.[134] Within the three years following the Act, a quarter of larger establishments had formal written redundancy agreements and by 1977 this figure had risen to a half of such establishments.[135]

The emphasis of legislation under full employment was for an improved utilization of manpower and a shake out of underutilized resources, particularly the skilled. Apart from redundancy compensation and statutory notice periods, there were no statutory restrictions on the deployment or dismissal of employees.

Labour legislation under growing unemployment

While many of the problems of low productivity, underutilization of labour and skill shortage persist, the growth of unemployment in the 1970s created a new backcloth against which labour laws would be enacted. Unfair dismissal provisions, originally conceived as the carrot to encourage trade unions to accept greater legal regulation of collective bargaining, became one aspect (along with employment subsidies and further restrictions on redundancy and lay-off) of a new policy aimed at protecting jobs and keeping people at work rather than on the unemployment register. We shall first consider the immediate impact of these new laws on organizations and then assess their longer term implications.

Redundancy payments legislation remains on the statute book but employers are finding the cost of redundancies increasing substantially. Recent surveys indicate that about 80 per cent of companies improve on the minimum compensation terms required by legislation. Such agreements include redundancy payments calculated on the basis of full service, additional allowances for age, the recognition of income in the calculation and payments for those below 18, above normal retirement age or with less than two years service. Estimates suggest that an employer's average redundancy payment is likely to be two or three times higher than that required by law.[136]

Not only are redundancies becoming increasingly costly for employers, but within an environment of rising unemployment, trade unions are increasingly resisting redundancies. A recent survey indicated that where trade unions existed, they had a strong influence on the method of manpower reduction adopted. Particularly, voluntary redundancy was preferred to enforced redundancy, with emphasis on measures to avoid redundancy: transfer; retraining; limiting recruitment; retiring those above retirement age; reduced overtime working; short-time working; dismissal of temporary workers. The survey indicated that 81 per cent of employer respondents had taken one or more of such initiatives to avoid declaring redundancies in the period 1974–77.[137]

Additionally, the concept of providing compensation for redundancy without any requirement to help employees find alternative employment or training has also been coming in for criticism. Daniel has criticized the Act for being the 'easiest and quickest way of doing something ... the "cash solution".' Britain, Daniel notes, is the only advanced industrial country in the world which makes statutory financial provision for employees when losing their jobs. He suggests that the emphasis should be placed on finding new employment for those displaced rather than cash sums of compensation, along the lines of Germany, France and Sweden.[138]

Any move in this direction would place a heavier responsibility on organizations, in conjunction with government agencies, for redundancy. Redundancy would become a more lengthy process since it could not take effect until individuals had found alternative work or commenced a course of retraining. As was mentioned in a previous section, current EEC proposals are likely to meet this kind of criticism by placing wider duties on the employer, which may include not only responsibility for retraining but a greater obligation to retrain and redeploy potentially redundant employees within the same organization. A further recent development has been the recognition by an organization of the social impact of redundancies and closures on some communities and the social responsibilities of the organization in such situations. The most notable example has been the British Steel Corporation which recognized the likely impact of closure and redundancy on communities almost entirely reliant on the steel industry for employment and where unemployment was already above the national average (for example, North-East England, Central Scotland and South Wales). Allowing a time scale of up to three years to effect closure, they were able to reduce the social impact, through liaison with government departments and agencies, to attract new industries to the sites of former steelworks and to arrange for the retraining where necessary of the existing workforce.[139]

If redundancy is becoming increasingly costly to organizations and may also as a concept be broadening to take into account redeployment, retraining and the social implications of closures, what about other forms of dismissal? Research suggests, as indicated in the table below, that unfair dismissal legislation as it currently exists has led to a sharp fall in the incidence of dismissal:[140]

Year	Proportion of employees dismissed in a 12 month period	Workplaces by numbers employed	
1969		100–499	500 or more
		%	%
	None	11	10
	1–5 per cent	76	84
	6–10 per cent	6	4
	11 per cent or more	7	2
		100	100

1977		100–499	500–999	1,000–5,000
		%	%	%
	None	18	15	8
	Less than 1 per cent	23	57	74
	1–3.4 per cent	48	17	13
	3.5 per cent or more	5	—	—
	Can't say	4	12	5
		100	100	100

Amongst smaller workplaces in 1969, seven per cent dismissed 11 per cent or more of their employees; by 1977, a small number (five per cent) dismissed only three and a half per cent or more. Amongst larger workplaces, the bulk of them in 1969 dismissed between one to five per cent of their workforce; by 1977, the tendency was a dismissal rate of less than one per cent of the workforce.

The new effect

One important conclusion can be drawn from the effects of this new restriction on redundancy and dismissal. Employees are ceasing to be the readily-disposable asset or the variable cost that they have been viewed as in the past. They are rapidly becoming a fixed element in the organization and once recruited are increasingly likely to remain a part of that organization until they resign of their own accord. This means that an employee, once recruited, may have to be trained, retrained, redeployed or transferred elsewhere within the organization much more than has been the case in the past.

Even more than before, the recruitment and selection process becomes increasingly critical. In addition to existing obligations to avoid discrimination on grounds of sex or race, we shall also be concerned that the new recruit is of the calibre required of those likely in all probability to become a permanent part of the organization. More important, we must become more concerned to assess the adaptability of candidates for the kind of retraining and redeployment that is increasingly being envisaged. These new developments therefore enhance the responsibilities of the personnel function and require a critical examination of the way current procedures are carried out. Although debate has surrounded the effects of recent employment legislation on rising unemployment, the real issue of importance to personnel managers is the effect of the legislation on professionally-competent personnel management practice. A recent survey suggests that it is in this respect that the impact of employment protection legislation has been greatest. In reply to questions on the impact of the new laws, the views of managers were summarized as follows:

The overwhelmingly most common answer was that unfair dismissal provisions had led management to reform, overhaul or formalize its internal procedures relating to disciplinary action, dismissals, grievances, selection, induction, the specification of terms and conditions of employment and so on.[141]

One or more of these changes were mentioned by 84 per cent of respondents. Apparently the Act had promoted attention to the human side of the enterprise and had encouraged management to take a more thorough, systematic and professional approach to this aspect of the business. Our conclusion that employees have tended to become fixed rather than variable elements in organizations can only further accelerate this process. The key role of the personnel manager within this will be considered again in the final part.

10

Education and working life

Chapter 6, on changes within the educational system, concluded that, from the statistical evidence at least, the educational attainments of younger entrants to the workforce were increasing at all levels. More people were achieving some examination passes before leaving school at the minimum age, more were undertaking sixth-form courses and more were entering and leaving the higher education system with degrees or other qualifications. This chapter aims to look at some current problems involved in bridging the transition between education and work and later the impact on organizations of possible future developments in the education/work relationship.

Current problems

In order to see where the problems lie, we must look at the respective expectations of employers and young people in relation to work and the extent to which there is a mismatch between the two. Employers are demanding competence in the basic skills of reading, writing, arithmetic, manual ability, the relevant technical skills or knowledge where applicable, some personal qualities related to ability to communicate and get on with others and an ability to exercise judgement or initiative. Also, employers are increasingly likely to expect a broader range of personal and process management skills rather than the narrower specialisms of the current education system, in order to facilitate flexibility and ability to retrain. Both of these are likely to become increasingly necessary during working life. Young people, for their part, because they have stayed at school longer, taken more qualifications and have been raised in a period of economic growth and rising mass consumption, have high expectations of both the intrinsic and extrinsic rewards of working life. As the OECD have recently put it:

> The expansion of education has raised the expectations and aspirations of many individuals for jobs and careers in which they can use their education and find wider opportunities for personal satisfaction and development.[142]

Now let us consider where the problems lie in the transition from school to work. There are three major reasons why reality is likely to differ from these expectations. The first arises from the state of the economy – low growth and rising unemployment. The second lies at the door of the employer and concerns the design of the jobs. The third lies partly with all other interested parties, employers, trade unions and government, and concerns the vocational preparation both within schools and after full-time education has finished.

Economic change

First, the slower rates of economic growth and higher rates of unemployment which are now occurring and are projected to continue, fall heavily upon young people entering the labour market for the first time. Therefore, far from meeting aspirations for intrinsically satisfying work, young people find it a struggle to get a job at all. Moreover, the slowing of economic growth means that the growth of organizations is also slowing down leaving less scope for promotion and advancement into more challenging work.

Job design

Secondly, there is the structure and design of jobs which young people, and indeed the workforce as a whole, are required to do. The problem has been put as follows:

> A basic contradiction in modern societies is that education for freedom and autonomy is followed, for many, by routine and boring work in hierarchic organizations. Consequently, the obverse of the need for education to provide a basis for employment is the need for jobs to be adapted to the aspirations of people.[143]

The implication of this is that if we educate people not only to higher standards of attainment but also by less formal or authoritarian methods to encourage initiative and an independent questioning approach, we cannot then expect people to be motivated in jobs which are routine and repetitive and in a working environment which expects unquestioning obedience to authority. On the one hand, we demand high standards of attainment, initiative and judgement, but on the other hand we cannot harness these qualities once we have them. Younger workers are increasingly critical of production line work, work in personal service occupations, low status work, menial or dirty tasks and manual work in general. This is evident in the difficulty in filling such vacancies even where unemployment is high. It is easy to be critical of such attitudes, it is a more difficult problem to examine the way jobs are designed, the work of groups is structured and the manner in which authority is devolved within organizations. This means of course reversing the trend of the last century which has progressively deskilled jobs by breaking them down into their smallest component parts, and decentralizing decision-making which has become concentrated at the top of large hierarchical organizations. In the words of one recent commentator, a failure to improve the match between aspirations or abilities and task requirements could induce 'excessive industrial unrest, social instability and significant decrements in the rate of technological/industrial progress.'[144]

Job redesign is not however only aimed at meeting social needs or aspirations but, as Chris Hayes has indicated, the case for it can be advanced on economic logic.[145] Improved vocational training and a wider base of skills and knowledge assists job redesign, indeed there is evidence from West Germany that it strongly influences work organization and job profiles. At the same time the economy benefits from a greater transferability of skills and a broader basis upon which to train in new skills when the situation so demands. Thus the challenge to industry is the urgent need to examine job design in order to utilize the additional capabilities, both creative and intellectual, of school leavers to the benefit of the individual, the organization and the economy as a whole.

A closer examination of job design is not only relevant when looking at jobs for school leavers, but is also critical when one recalls the projected growth of 'highly qualified' persons; that is those with first degrees or equivalent qualifications, expected to enter the labour market in the 1980s.

The labour market of the 1950s and 1960s was generally very favourable to the highly qualified. They were much in demand, a relatively scarce commodity and were well-paid. In effect, the availablility of places in higher education expanded to meet the demands of young people more rapidly than the demands for such people expanded in the labour market. In the last few years the employment prospects for graduates have become less favourable. One of the main findings of a recent study of the employment prospects facing graduates during the next few years indicates that the availability of jobs traditionally held by graduates will not expand sufficiently to meet the projected increase in the output of them.[146] Between 1971 and 1986, the output of graduates is expected to increase by almost 100 per cent while the number of jobs traditionally taken by graduates will increase by only 50 per cent.

The table below shows a relatively predictable pattern of graduate employment in 1971 with the bulk employed in managerial, professional and technical jobs, although nearly seven per cent in clerical and sales.

Table 18
Percentage of highly qualified by occupation (GB) 1971

Occupation	% Highly qualified
Clerical workers	3.7
Sales workers	3.1
Administrators and managers	11.6
Professional, technical workers, artists }	76.9
All other occupations	4.7
	100.00

The next table gives some indication of how this pattern might be expected to change.

The projections emphasize that opportunities in traditional jobs will grow by only about half the increase in graduate numbers between 1971 and 1986. Within these traditional jobs, the biggest expansion is amongst clerical workers, but more significantly, half the graduates of 1986 will be looking for jobs completely

112

outside these traditional occupations. As the report points out: 'Jobs which twenty years ago were not considered suitable for or by graduates are now widely accepted as appropriate for graduate employees.'[147]

Table 19
Occupational distribution of the estimated number of jobs of the kind held by graduates in 1971, likely to be available in 1986 (GB)

Occupation	% Increase 1971–1986
Clerical workers	61
Sales workers	23
Administrators and managers	38
Professional, technical workers, artists }	52
All other occupations	28
ALL OCCUPATIONS	49

The performance by graduates of a whole range of jobs at the lower end of the organizational hierarchy, including clerical, technical, and possibly manual tasks has important implications both for the redesign of the immediate job in question and for jobs above and below it in the organizational hierarchy. Certainly, recent years have seen some changes in recruitment patterns. Graduates are now being increasingly recruited for jobs done in the past by good 'A' level school-leavers – for example, management traineeships. The Civil Service has recently witnessed an expansion of graduates in clerical and higher clerical employment. A recent intake of Executive Officers consisted of 50 per cent graduates, 10 years ago the figure would have been nearer five per cent.

These changing patterns are not peculiar to Britain. A similar situation has been reported in the USA, Canada and Sweden, where the graduate employment markets have been characterized by growing unemployment, lengthened job searches and a decline in the relative earnings of new graduates.[148] Similar experiences have also been reported in Italy, the Netherlands and to some extent in France. As in Britain, higher education has expanded in response to the demand for places rather than the demands of the labour market, with the result that graduates have had to revise their employment expectations downwards.[149]

There are therefore many facets to the role of job redesign in organizations and this is an issue to which we shall return in part IV.

Vocational training

The third major problem area adding to the difficulties of the transfer from education to working life is the role of vocational training both within the school system and after it. Currently, elements of vocational education for young people are divided between the education system, government and employers. The system is a fragmented one: the quality and quantity of vocational education in the school curricula varies from establishment to establishment, some school leavers are entering one or other of an increasing range of work experience programmes sponsored by government and a further number are entering craft or technical training courses. Many employers are critical of the over-academic emphasis in the school curricula at the secondary school level, the lack of understanding, experience or sympathy of many teachers to work in industry and an inadequate provision within schools of career guidance or information. Employers are also critical of the fragmented and often complex system of job creation and work experience programmes for school leavers. Educationists for their part argue that they are aiming to provide a broad education for life, the concept of a traditional liberal education, rather than training for young people in specific skills. Current hopes are that some of these areas of difference can be closed: on the one hand school curricula will shift to provide a better preparation for adult life, including work, while at the same time a more comprehensive post-school programme of education and training is likely to be developed, with the government and employers sharing responsibility for vocational preparation and employers responsible for occupational training. Such a period of, say, one of two years following the leaving of school at the minimum age could serve a number of useful purposes: remedy deficiencies in basic educational skills, provide for work experience, allow further time for career decisions and generally assist in adjusting aspirations on transition from school to work. Such a system has worked in Germany where, following the completion of nine years compulsory schooling at age 15, compulsory part-time vocational schooling continues for three years for those not continuing full-time education. Any such extended system of vocational preparation in Britain would inevitably involve employing organizations. Since young people represent the workforce of tomorrow, it is right that employers should be involved. As one report has recently concluded:

> It is to the advantage of employers to adapt their employment structures and recruitment policies to provide more opportunities for part-time or temporary jobs and to create 'entry' jobs that offer work experience of longer-term value to young recruits.[150]

Future developments

For two major reasons, education is expected to play a more significant role throughout people's lives in the future. First, because the increasing pace of technological change will accelerate the obsolescence of skills and increase the need for training and retraining. Secondly, the long-term tendency for leisure time to increase is likely to involve education in expanding out-of-work activities.

The first of these reasons is of most relevance to this chapter and it is increasingly being argued that a policy of 'recurrent' or 'continuous' education and training is becoming appropriate to meet economic, social and labour market objectives.[151] Six main arguments are put forward in support of this concept:

Obsolescence: more frequent education and training will be required not only to assist those in jobs to meet changing skill requirements, but also those out of work as a result of structural changes. From a national manpower perspective, recurrent education and training can assist in meeting shortages in certain skills.

Flexibility: currently the acquisition of a body of knowledge occurs at the beginning of the career and largely determines the occupation throughout working life. It is argued that under a system based on rapid change, more flexibility to change career mid-stream, involving a return to full-time education, is increasingly required.

Motivation: it is argued that the current pattern involving years of continuous education during youth can have detrimental effects leading to poor motivation during, or on completion of studies and 'dropping out'. Recurrent education and training could alleviate this problem by permitting more opportunities to return to full-time study later in life.

Special education programmes: the coming of participation is bringing with it the need to expand educational programmes in order that those participating might do so effectively. Any development of 'worker director' proposals ought to consider the educational implications of the notion.

Adult education: as a result of improvements in the educational system, each generation of school leavers experiences greater educational opportunities than the previous one. The result is that the older segment of the workforce is considerably disadvantaged, a balance which can to some extent be re-dressed by continuous education.

Forecasting difficulties: as a result of swift social and technological changes, forecasting labour market needs and aligning these to educational output is becoming increasingly difficult. The rapid creation of new knowledge and its swift application, together with shifts in trading conditions both internal and external to a national economy make this so and provide further justification for recurrent education to adjust man-power deficiencies.

As regards future developments, it is possible that legislation may be extended into this area if practice in Europe is taken as an indicator. In France, a law of 1971 allowed for up to two per cent of a firm's labour force to be away on educational leave of absence and the scheme is financed by a levy/grant system operated by the state. A Belgian law of 1973 created a 'credit d'heures' system enabling employees under 40 to spend up to 10 days a year on training or educational courses and also pro-vided the right for those studying in the evening to be absent from work, on full pay, for a certain number of hours. In Germany, various federal states have passed legislation since 1974 allowing five to 10 days educational leave per year. In Italy, the collective agreements of most industrial sectors make provision for educational leave.[152] A proposal on 'worksharing' by the EEC Commission includes paid study-leave as a means of reducing pressure in the labour market.

In conclusion, rising educational attainment and the growing need for employees at all levels to train and retrain during their

116

working life means that education and working life will come closer together. This means a behavioural change on the part of both educationists and employers. The education system at all levels will need to adapt to cater for the future job requirements of all those whom they teach and at the same time, at the tertiary level, continue to expand flexibly programmed courses to meet the growing demand for recurrent education. Employing organizations for their part will be required to become more actively involved in occupational training and work experience programmes for young people and also to appraise critically aspects of the quality of working life, particularly the design of jobs.

Part four

SUMMARY AND IMPLICATIONS

11

Summary

The book has sought to show that organizations and the problems which they face have many of their origins in the complex and changing environment in which they operate. The major aspects of change currently facing organizations may now be summarized:

Economic: for two decades or more, organizations were able to operate within an economic climate of relatively high rates of economic growth, an expanding demand for the goods and services produced, assisted by low levels of unemployment. Such an economic environment, while generating wealth and raising the living standards of the population to an unprecedented extent, was not without its problems. Particularly, full employment created tight labour markets which in turn contributed to some of the major problems of the 1950s and 1960s – skill shortage, the underutilization of manpower, low productivity and the emergence of trade union bargaining at plant level within the context of an industrial relations system formally based on national negotiations. While many of the problems arising from this framework persist, recent experience and future projections indicate a slowing of past rates of economic growth with unemployment persisting at levels higher than were experienced during this 25 year growth period. The effect of this is that most organizations are not expecting to expand in the way they have in the past, with all the implications this has for career prospects, job security and redundancy. Organizations will continue to be concerned with such problems as productivity and manpower utilization in order to remain competitive, but at the same time will be faced with the contrary pressures of employees to avoid redundancies, meet promotional expectations and adopt measures such as worksharing to spread available work in the face of high unemployment.

Demographic: at the same time as a less favourable economic climate is preventing the expansion of jobs, so more people will actually be looking for them in the next few years as a result of an expansion in the size of the labour force. Although this is in part chance, it is also a product of the affluence generated in the earlier period. Rising aspirations for more material wealth and the changing role of women has attracted many more women into the labour market. Affluence probably also led to the rise in birth rates in the late 1950s and 1960s resulting in an increase in the number of young people coming on to the labour market both currently and over the next few years. Not only has the rise in the working population coincided with a fall in the availability of jobs, but the problem of unemployment has been compounded by its effect on these rising numbers of young people leading to a range of government measures to alleviate the problem.

Social: full employment and rising living standards led the expectations and aspirations of people at work to rise correspondingly. People continue to expect job security and rises in living standards. This is so even within a context of low economic growth that makes it more difficult for organizations to meet these aspirations when they themselves are faced with a low growth in demand for their goods or services.

Structural: at the same time as the general economic climate is prohibiting the expansion of jobs, many large employers of labour in the manufacturing sector of industry, particularly in Britain but also in other countries, are in decline. This is part of a longer term shift in employment which has led to a fall in employment in the manufacturing industry and a growth in the service sector. This is also leading to a shift in the types of skills demanded, from manual to non-manual, particularly technical, professional and managerial skills. On the one hand the traditional employers of unskilled and semi-skilled labour are offering fewer employment opportunities. On the other hand the further expansion of the public service sector, which might have offered alternative employment opportunities, is now constrained by the low rates of growth facing the economy as a whole.

Technical: technological change and its accompanying problems of obsolete skills and the need to retrain in new ones have for a long time been an integral part of industrial development. Recent technological developments, particularly in the field of microelectronics, could bring about changes in working life which are substantially different from our more recent experience of the impact of technological change. Microelectronic computer technology is likely to play an important role in substantially raising industrial productivity, as well as the quality and reliability of the goods produced, but at the same time is likely to have a wide-reaching impact on the workforce at all levels in the organization. It is likely to form the basis of management information, communication and control systems bringing about significant changes in the structure of management jobs, further extend the automation of jobs performed by secretarial and clerical employees and have wide reaching effects on the manual sector of the workforce, calling for the upgrading of the skills of many craft-level employees while reducing the demand in the unskilled and semi-skilled groups. The possibilities are that it could further contribute to the upward trend in unemployment which is already occurring because of changes in the economic climate and, although the extent to which this may happen is open to debate, there is little doubt that the potential effects of this technology on the workforce are far reaching. Given however the doubts that surround job security with a context of already high levels of unemployment, the negotiation and implementation of such technological change will be that much more difficult.

Legal: the growth of legal intervention in the British system of industrial relations, augmenting the traditional 'voluntarist' or non-interventionist role of law, occurred from the 1960s onwards in response to problems within the economic system. The problems of an economic growth rate below that of our competitors, periodic balance of payments difficulties and a tendency for the economy to inflate at full employment were diagnosed as stemming from deficiencies in the industrial relations system. The background was one of full employment and labour shortage and the major problems were manpower underutilization, skill shortage and more specific industrial relations problems – the inflationary nature of plant bargaining and unofficial strikes. The labour laws of the 1960s and early 1970s were, in their various ways, aimed at alleviating some of these problems. Since many of these problems still exist these laws remain on the statute book, but the legislation of the past few years should be seen in a different context. The background is now one of growing unemployment and many of the recent measures have been aimed at keeping people in work rather than on the unemployment register. Tighter unfair dismissal regulations, the range of measures contained in the Employment Protection Act and a range of labour subsidies, including the Temporary Employment Subsidy and special measures for young people, may all be seen within this framework. Redundancies and rationalization, encouraged in the 1960s, are now not as actively encouraged as they once were and the attitude of trade unions towards them is hardening. Effectively what is happening, with a fall in the rate of dismissal and opposition to redundancy, is that employees are ceasing to be the readily disposable assets of organizations which they once were. They are becoming fixed assets which, once recruited, are likely to remain with the organization longer, particularly the less skilled or less qualified. The onus is therefore increasingly on the organization to select less narrowly for a specific vacancy, to train, retrain, redeploy or otherwise utilize the people which it already employs.

Educational: the educational standards of the workforce are rising at all levels from the school leaver to the graduate. Their aspirations have also risen – for more intrinsically interesting work, for an opportunity to participate in decisions which affect them and for many, the opportunity for promotion and advancement with the organization. But the economic forces of low growth and rising unemployment constrain these aspirations. If organizations are not expanding, there are fewer opportunities since not only will fewer people be recruited but also fewer opportunities since not only will fewer people be recruited but also fewer opportunities will arise for promotion and advancement within the organization. Perhaps the widest gap between expectations and reality is being experienced by graduates. Once a scarce commodity very much in demand, they are now less scarce and are not able to command the initial appointments, salaries and job expectations which they once could. Graduates are now taking up appointments at much lower levels in the organization than formerly. Generally rising educational standards have been accompanied by a general upward revision within organizations of the qualifications required for jobs at each level. At the same time attention has not always been paid to the content of jobs given to increasingly better qualified job holders.

In conclusion, the overall picture is one of conflicting pressures in the environment facing organizations when adapting to meet the needs of the new situation. It should be stressed that these various aspects of change should not be seen in isolation but as part of an integrated whole with any one area of change having a bearing on the others. It is for this reason that the combination of changes outlined are in many ways unique and as a whole present a new and different picture facing personnel departments. Economic difficulties and a rise in the working population are causing unemployment which may create obstacles to the adoption of technological change vital to the future of British industry, and the wider framework of structural change in industry further compounds these fears of insecurity and unemployment. The rising aspirations born of educational and social change conflict with the realities of a low growth economy in respect of wage and salary expectations, promotional opportunities and overall job security.

Finally, organizations are faced with the problem of raising productivity and adopting new technology in order to remain viable, while at the same time are finding it increasingly difficult and costly, as a result of legislation, to declare redundancies, dismiss, or otherwise reduce manning levels in order to achieve higher productivity. Since these problems all concern the way organizations use human resources, the development of sound personnel policies is a key way in which organizations can adapt to meet these new problems.

12

Some implications
for personnel specialists

This section aims to show how personnel policies can assist in meeting these new problems. They are not intended as panaceas which may be applied as a package to all organizations, but should be considered more in the light of the particular problems faced in a given situation. The policy measures are not in themselves new but are intended to illustrate how measures currently available to personnel managers might be viewed in the light of the changes identified in this book. To avoid going over previously well-covered ground, the measures themselves are not described in enormous detail, but the reader who may wish to familiarize himself further is recommended in the references to publications appropriate to this task.[153]

Personnel planning

Planning in the context of personnel policies is sometimes associated with the sophisticated mathematical and statistical models of the manpower planner. For many personnel practitioners it is an activity quite separate from his own function, a specialist activity of which he knows little and cares less. Recent years however have seen a change in emphasis in the role of manpower planning. The manpower planner is still concerned with the quantitative and qualitative measurement of manpower needs in organizations in relation to corporate objectives, but with less emphasis on mathematical modelling. Rising employment costs and the emergence of people at work as 'fixed assets' make clear the critical importance of effective company manpower planning in order to control these costs and to recruit the number and calibre of employees needed to meet longer term objectives rather than short-term expediencies. The manpower planner is also increasingly concerned with the wider aspects of change in the environment, as discussed in this book, and their effects on the personnel policies, and it is in this latter area that the active involvement of all personnel managers is felt to be an essential part of implementing change within organizations. Reference was made earlier to pressures, particularly trade union pressures, for worksharing and the implications for the organization as a whole of such measures should be assessed now rather than when the pressures become more urgent. A major question concerning the reduction of man hours available through such worksharing measures as cuts in the working week, overtime cuts, extra holidays and so on are their effects on the organization's demand for manpower in order to maintain existing levels of output. This may require the recruitment of new employees and our concern will be whether replacements of the calibre and skill required are available in the labour market. Early retirement may lead to the loss of key senior personnel whom we might want to replace from inside the organization. Our concern would then be with our stock of trained and experienced replacements. On the other hand, it may be possible to maintain output levels without further recruitment by raising labour productivity through changes in working arrangements, more flexible working or the replacement of high overtime levels by shiftworking. Many other problems are likely to be encountered with the concept of worksharing. Overtime for example may have been used periodically to meet trade peaks or carry out periodic tasks such as cleaning or machine maintenance. Any general cut in overtime would create problems here. We may consider the recruitment of contractors or temporary staff, exploiting the growing market supply of temporary workers, part-timers and double jobholders. At the same time, recruiting such employees may have disruptive effects on industrial relations, pay systems and differentials. Any solution requires an assessment of these possible conflicts. The introduction of shiftwork also requires some important manpower decisions. Particularly, is the calibre of new recruit available in the labour market and prepared to do shiftwork? Also what is the likely reaction of our current work force to shiftworking? Any loss of key personnel, particularly managerial or technical, would seriously impair productive efficiency. To take a final example, the sharing of one job by two people could be used to solve particular manpower problems. It could be used as part of an early retirement strategy or where recruitment problems exist (for example, the employment part-time of two women with family commitments to share one job). The problems associated with this need also to be thought out, not least the communication with and between job holders. Indeed all the costs and difficulties associated with worksharing need careful consideration and analysis in order to ascertain what the organizational implications of them might be.

Not only do personnel managers need to become increasingly involved in a planning approach to personnel decisions but they also need to get involved in the strategic planning decisions of the organization as a whole. The manner in which this is done will depend on how the organization formulates such policies and takes decisions. In very large organizations it is likely to be associated with the corporate planning department, in others such policies are likely to be formulated at board level, or indeed may not be formally expressed at all. Wherever and however such policies are planned, it is important that personnel functions not only involve but also clearly demonstrate the value of their contribution. This would include the behavioural, manpower and industrial relations implications of the proposed changes together with an analysis of the likely costs and benefits of adopting one decision as against another. The overall aim must be to improve the effectiveness of corporate planning and decision making and avoid the all too frequent situation in which personnel functions are left to 'fire-fight' the manpower and industrial relations effects of decisions to which they have not been a part. This becomes particularly important in the context of the planning and implementation of technological change. As Mumford has argued:

> When firms are planning for the introduction of new techno-logical systems . . . concentration on technical and economic variables can be a major defect for it can lead to a lack of planning for important variables in the personnel and human relations area.[154]

It was argued earlier that different types of technology are closely associated with social systems within organizations and a change in the former can affect the skills required, job content, social interrelationships, promotion prospects and job security within the latter. The implications of technical change need to be thought through in advance in order that plans can be made for reductions in numbers or retraining in new skills, *before* changes take place, in order to minimize the impact and potential for conflict. Plans for implementing change should also allow sufficient time for consultation, communication and retraining which are key aspects of successful implementation. Where the implementation of change is likely to have a major effect on the future employment prospects of a community, workforce resistance is likely to be greater and an adequate time scale may have to be allowed to enable liaison with public authorities in attracting new employment to the locality. Whatever the nature of the change proposed, if it has implications for the human resource within organizations, a lack of involvement by the personnel function at an early stage in the overall planning process must mean that personnel managers will continue to 'fire-fight' reactively to change rather than proactively influencing the process of change itself.[155]

Career planning

Although part of the personnel planning process, the questions raised by a low growth economy for careers and career planning are sufficiently significant to merit separate treatment. The career prospects in any individual organization are related to the rates of wastage and the age structure of the workforce. But across the economy as a whole low rates of economic growth mean that organizations will also grow less slowly and opportunities for promotion and advancement will reduce. The effect is also likely to be proportionately greater since the growth of unemployment and the attendant feelings of insecurity which it creates, together with the effect of employment protection legislation, mean that generally throughout the economy the number of job changes will fall and indeed have already begun to do so.[156] A number of problems emerge from this new situation. Poorer career prospects may have an adverse effect on the motivation of younger employees who expect part of their reward to come in the form of promotion. This may lead to dissatisfaction and the 'high flyers' amongst them, whose services are sought after, may well leave, posing problems for the future calibre of the organization's management team. On the other hand, creating more career opportunities for younger executives would mean the redundancy of older ones with all the implications this has for organizational age structure, the experience of the management team, the cost of such redundancies and ultimately the motivation of management as a whole.

While the fundamental problem of upward advancement is one to which there is no ready answer within an economic environment of low growth, there are a number of measures which are worthy of consideration. First, it may be that the assumption that all people doing jobs normally associated with upward career moves actually want promotion should be challenged. While there are many people who will have such aspirations, there may be others who do not want to progress beyond a certain point but feel obliged to accept promotion because of the organizational situation in which they find themselves. Secondly, the general notion of career may need to be broadened to take in some form of job rotation. This would mean a series of horizontal rather than vertical moves designed to broaden experience and provide new responsibilities and job interest, but at basically similar levels in the organization, before there is further upward movement. Thirdly, organizations may have to increasingly create posts, perhaps for a limited period of time, to provide alternative job interest. Fourthly, organizations may have to consider redesigning or enlarging the responsibilities of existing posts to develop interest and motivation. Fifthly, the extension of participation might be considered not only in the context of improving industrial relations but also as a means of involving middle management more fully in the decision-making of the organization as a whole. Finally, given the accelerating pace of change, be it technical, social or whatever, it may mean that an even more extensive review of the concept of careers is called for. Where up-to-date technical knowledge is vital to job success, swift advancement may occur early in the career followed by slower movement later in life. Alternatively, careers may be characterized by periodic breaks in order to return to full-time education to update skills and knowledge or to acquire a completely new set of skills before moving up the organizational hierarchy. Whatever policies will be implemented in relation to careers and career planning, they seem unlikely to follow in the future the traditional patterns of the past.

Recruitment and selection

Legal restrictions on the 'right to hire and fire' and with it the emergence of the employee as a fixed rather than variable asset with the onus on the organization to develop and utilize that asset, means that the recruitment and selection process has now become even more critical. This is the point of entry for new employees, employees who are likely to remain much longer within the organization and may have to be retrained in the future for new tasks or in new skills. This is likely to involve a re-examination of job descriptions and employee specifications in the light of future projected job changes in the organization and a revision of some recruitment requirements. Many employee specifications refer to the need for the quality of 'adaptability' or more positively 'versatility', and this quality in employees is likely to take on increasing importance. Clearly, isolating any particular trait in a potential employee presents difficult problems, but some indications of qualities such as versatility and flexibility might emerge in an interview, perhaps in the candidate's previous job history (evidence of skill transferability, for example), or education, or through the use of psychological tests. Whatever steps are taken, the need for careful selection and recruitment is paramount and needs to take place within a clear framework of change in the organization as a whole.

Negotiating change

Since trade union attitudes are hardening against redundancy within a framework of rising unemployment, management is having to adopt a longer time scale when planning and implementing change, particularly technological change. As argued above, all too frequently personnel departments have been involved at the implementation phase but not in the planning, yet the possibility of increasing trade union opposition to the declaration of redundancy must be an important reason for the involvement of the personnel department in examining the manpower and industrial relations effects of new technology at the earliest possible stage. Unions also are increasingly demanding early involvement in various stages of the planning process and the view has been expressed that 'there can be little doubt that in some industries this has a favourable effect on the implementation and planning of change'.[157] Finally, discussions should also involve the line management likely to be affected by the change and all discussions should take place at the plant or location where the change will occur.

Planning in advance will assist in avoiding redundancies and allow a period of time over which to effect manpower reductions. This is likely to include a halt to recruitment, with short term needs being met through the use of temporary staff, some loss through natural wastage, transfer or relocation, early retirement and retraining programmes. Where new technology forces the closure of a whole plant, then organizations may increasingly be called upon to perform a wider social function, in cooperation with government agencies, by assisting further in placing people in new jobs, retraining or attracting new investment to the location.

Wage systems and job evaluation

The view that 'wage systems do not function in isolation from their technological, economic and social settings'[158] is an important one and echoes the view expressed in earlier chapters that what happens inside organizations is very much a product of the environment in which they operate. Lupton and Gowler have developed a 'contingency' approach to selecting the most appropriate wage payment system dependent upon a number of key factors in the organization's environment.[159] These key factors are technology, the labour market, the effectiveness of the disputes procedure and some structural characteristics of the industry including the nature of the unionization, age structure of the workforce and the ratio of labour cost to total cost.

Two of these factors are particularly relevant in the light of our previous discussion. Technology is likely to have an important influence on payment systems because the nature of the technology determines the kind of skills which an organization will require. Where the prevailing technology is not highly automated (such as in craft or machine systems) the individual worker has significant control over the pace of work. In such situations, payment systems such as 'payment by results' or 'piecework' have frequently been applied. Where the degree of automation is higher and level of individual control over the work pace lower (as in automated production lines, process or computerized technology), such a payment system is not usually appropriate. Given that the new technological developments referred to ⟨ea⟩ier indicate a move in the latter direction, so it is likely that ⟨⟩ employees will move towards a fixed salary for a broad ⟨⟩f responsibility rather than pay related to output, pay ⟨⟩ bears little relationship to the input of effort within a highly automated system.

An important influence of the local labour market on the payment system is its degree of 'tightness' which causes recruitment difficulties as a result of labour shortage. It was earlier argued that post-war full employment and consequently 'tight' labour markets led both to employers bidding up wages against each other and to unions using plant bargaining power to augment this process. The rise of unemployment might be expected to lessen pressure in local labour markets and relax this process. There is no evidence so far that higher levels of unemployment have reduced trade union bargaining power in the plant. Moreover, the persisting shortage of particular skills, even within a framework of high unemployment, will continue to mean competition in the labour market for certain categories of employee.

Turning now to systems of job evaluation, which may be defined as the processes of determining an orderly and equitable relationship between jobs in a pay structure, these too are open to the wider influences of change in and around organizations. Technological change, for example, can change the traditional relationship between jobs, by reducing the skill content of some jobs through mechanization while upgrading other jobs by adding to their responsibility element. Job evaluation schemes depend on a weighting given to particular factors. An increase in automation is likely to shift this weighting from such factors as physical effort or working conditions and towards mental effort and responsibility. As Stieber has argued:

> In general the newer job standards are geared more to the qualifications and training of the worker than to his performance . . . Many are paid for what they *may* be required to do.[160]

A failure to reappraise an existing job evaluation structure in the light of technological change is likely to lead to a 'bunching' of jobs in the higher grades and a destruction of felt-fair differentials.

Job redesign

Reference has already been made to the rising aspirations and qualifications of leavers from the educational system and particular reference was made to the increasing number of graduates entering the world of work during the next few years. At the same time it was suggested that a number of factors existed which were tending to frustrate these aspirations and to lead to an underutilization of individual potential. First, organizations were growing little in the framework of a low growth economy and were therefore offering fewer initial job opportunities and poorer promotion prospects. Secondly, because of higher standards of education in the workforce, organizations have been able to increase at all levels the qualifications required on entry, from the 16 year old school leaver to the first class honours graduate, while at the same time recruiting these new entrants at relatively lower levels in the organizational hierarchy.

The general effect is that today's graduate does the job of yesterday's 'A' level school leaver; today's 'A' level school leaver takes a job formerly requiring 'O' levels only and those with little or no qualifications find it increasingly hard to find a job at all. The result of this conflict of attainment and aspiration with reality is likely to lead to problems of frustration and poor motivation. Job redesign, that is a reassessment of the range of tasks performed and the level of responsibility for decision-making permitted, is a useful way of broadening job content to meet the capabilities of the job holder and of enabling the organization to make more effective use of those capabilities.[161] As mentioned in the context of career planning, job enlargement by widening responsibilties or job rotation are variations on this theme which may also prove useful given the problems of promotion blockage.

New automated technology could further aggravate this process. New technical systems designed and installed by technical experts are aimed at the maximum efficiency of operation in which the human being is a necessary extension of the technical process. There is nothing new in this. We are familiar with F. W. Taylor's concept of the 'economic man.[162] and McGregor's 'Theory X'.[163] But the personnel manager might argue that a concept of maximum efficiency which fails to take into account the perceptions, attitudes and motivation of the people expected to work with the new technology cannot square with reality. A technically highly efficient system is unlikely to produce the expected gains in productivity if those who work amidst the new technology have no motivation to make that system work effectively. With the growth of automation, both in the factory and the office, it is important to analyse the potential of the new technology for routinizing work and, perhaps with the assistance of interviews or attitude surveys, reconstruct around the new technology those elements of the job which motivate people. It should be stressed that we are not just talking about factory or clerical jobs but, as was discussed earlier, all jobs up to at least middle management level, all of which are likely to be affected by automation. This means actively conniving against all those aspects of new technology which increase monotony, repetitiveness and lack of discretion with the overall objective of raising organizational efficiency by increasing individual satisfaction.

Reference was also made earlier to the need for greater versatility and transferability of skill on the part of employees in order to meet change. Highly fragmented work systems do little to develop such versatility and indeed stifle any versatility which an employee may have begun to acquire.

Participation

This is not the appropriate place to enter into a long discussion of participation which has, in any case, been very fully treated by literature on the subject.[164] It is worth, however, highlighting its role in connection with the aspects of change identified in this book. Before continuing it should be emphasized that job redesign is the most direct way of increasing individual involvement with his job, without any other machinery or institutions. By increasing responsibility and involvement in decision-making related to the immediate environment of the job, greater participation in organizational affairs is immediately effected.

Having said this, there may be broader organizational decisions, investment plans, marketing changes, product changes, technical changes, which may benefit from some wider process of consultation. Here of course is the problem of reconciling the difficulties of involving each and every individual with some sort of representative system which affords any meaningful partipation at all for the majority – the classical dilemma of nearly all democratic systems. Representative institutions such as participative or consultative committees can be augmented by a system of briefing groups to enhance individual participation and this may be one approach to overcoming the dilemma. Whichever of the range of participative structures selected, our main concern here is to see how participation, in its various forms, might assist in resolving some of the problems identified earlier. Where technological change is proposed, participation may assist the process of planning and implementation. Where career structures are blocked, participation may provide a means of broadening and enlarging jobs which people may be required to hold for some time. Where educational attainments and aspirations are not being satisfied within the job itself, participation may enhance job interest. Together, job redesign and other structures of participation can therefore play an important part in helping organizations to adapt to a changing environment.

Training and development

Implicit in what has been said already is the central and increasing role of training and retraining in helping organizations to adapt effectively to changed conditions. Some reference has already been made to the problems of career planning in a low growth organizational and economic framework, and similar problems may be applied to management development. Recent research has suggested that career advancement is *the* criterion upon which managers base their decisions about leaving or staying in organizations, but it has been argued that:

> It is difficult to escape the conclusion that management development in large organizations will only operate effectively if the organization is growing and that, conversely, growth is the best solution to management development problems.[165]

The major conclusion need only briefly be restated. In the absence of the traditional motivation involving upward career movement, secondments, job rotation or job enlargement need increasingly to be considered. Development programmes will increasingly require more training to counter the effects of obsolescence, which is likely to occur more rapidly than in the past, not only as a result of technical change, but also as a result of the changing social, political and economic climate in which change is occurring.

On a broader front, the combination of technical change and legal restrictions against redundancy and dismissal will mean that organizations will increasingly be required to utilize their existing employees by developing their current skills and by retraining them in new ones. The 'skills' which people possess should not however be viewed too narrowly. A glance at some of the employment legislation over just the last five years indicates the importance of training to develop the broad skills of *all* employees with regard to health and safety, discrimination, participation, human relations and the whole range of socio-legal

136

obligations which underlie how we all approach our jobs.

It seems most appropriate to conclude our discussion by posing questions about what needs to be done *now* in order to help prepare all our organizations for the new conditions which are emerging:

Do we know what the organization's longer term plans and objectives are?

Have we made a personal contribution to these plans by highlighting the human resource problems, both internal and external, which have been discussed in this book?

Have we examined the costs and organizational implications of these changes?

Have we discussed these broad issues of change and their likely impact on the organization with fellow managers, foremen, other employees and the trade union representatives?

Are we making decisions and taking action **now** *in order to meet these planned organizational objectives?*

During the next decade, the nature of the changes facing those responsible for managing people at work are likely to be fundamentally different from those experienced during the last 30 years. Lower rates of economic growth, rising levels of unemployment and substantial technical change may conflict with the traditional aspirations of employees for rising standards of living and guaranteed security of employment. Living and managing with change has taken on more meaning than the glib and over-used epithet that it has tended to become. Closer attention is now needed by managers to the emerging labour market problems which this book has sought to outline in relation to their own organization's policies. This will assist organizations in achieving both their current and future objectives and at the same time maximize the use of the human resources available to them in doing so.

Appendix

A brief review of recent measures to reduce unemployment is as follows:

Temporary Employment Subsidy

This was introduced in August 1975 with the objective of deferring impending redundancies of 10 or more workers. The scheme basically offers a £20 per week subsidy, payable for a maximum of 12 months, for each full-time job maintained. In certain instances a further supplement of £10 per week per worker is also available. About three-fifths of current payments go to protecting jobs in the textile, clothing and footwear industries, which did arouse some criticism from the EEC because of its distorting effect on competition.

Job Release Scheme

This was introduced in January 1977 to enable employees within one year of statutory pension age to retire and make way for a registered unemployed person. The scheme applied to assisted areas only, but since April 1978 it has been extended to cover the whole country and currently provides the taker with £26.50 tax free per week.

Special Temporary Employment Programme (formerly the Job Creation Programme)

The Job Creation Programme started in October 1975 and aimed at providing full-time temporary employment on projects which benefit the community for people who would otherwise be unemployed. From autumn 1978 this became the Special Temporary Employment Programme, which will provide 25,000 temporary jobs for those aged 19–24 who have been unemployed for a year or more. Each person is allowed a maximum of one year on the scheme and will be paid an agreed rate for the job.

Youth Opportunities Programme (formerly the Work Experience Programme)

The Work Experience Programme started in October 1976 and involved an introduction to working life on employers premises for the young unemployed between 16 and 18. The young people concerned receive a £16 weekly allowance. This programme was expanded last autumn under the Youth Opportunities Programme to provide a programme of employment induction courses followed by short industrial courses related to the skills needed in specific occupational areas. The programme is available to young people under 19 who have been unemployed for six weeks or more and all unemployed school leavers. Each year this scheme is designed to provide 234,000 places plus jobs for 8,000 unemployed adults as supervisors and young people will be paid £19.50 per week free of tax and national insurance.

Community Industry

This scheme, introduced as a temporary measure in 1972, is run by the National Association of Youth Clubs with government funding to provide for disadvantaged young people.

Youth Employment Subsidy

This was introduced in October 1976 and is aimed at young people under 20 who have been unemployed for six months or more and provides employers with a subsidy of £10 for up to 26 weeks for every young person taken on.

Job Introduction Scheme For Disabled Persons

Introduced in July 1977, it is aimed at helping certain disabled
140

people who have been out of work for at least six months. A subsidy of £30 for a trial six weekly period will be paid to employers, but only in circumstances where the employers have some prior reasonable doubt about the ability of the disabled person to perform the job.

Small Firms Employment Subsidy

Introduced on an experimental basis in July 1977, the scheme currently provides a subsidy for manufacturing firms in the private sector with 50 employees or less of £20 per week for up to 26 weeks for each extra job created. Currently the scheme applies to firms in Special Development areas with 200 employees or less and also applies in all Assisted Areas, including the Inner City Partnership Areas, including the London Docklands and inner Birmingham.

Details of the two training measures in operation are as follows:

Special training courses for young people

Government-sponsored training run by the Manpower Services Commission (MSC) for young people began in 1971 and has expanded rapidly since 1975. Courses include occupational selection and short industrial courses developing skills at the semi-skilled level. During 1976 over 15,000 young people were trained under these programmes.

Special measures to maintain training opportunities with employers for young people

These schemes are funded by MSC and administered mainly through the Industrial Training Boards over and above the levy/grant/exemption schemes. During 1976 over 40,000 places were made available.

Table 20
Summary of numbers affected and cost of these measures

	Total no who have benefited	Cost 1976/77 £m	Cost 1977/78 £m
Temporary Employment Subsidy	371,100	92.4	200.0
Job Release Scheme	21,500	1.6	16.5
Job Creation Programme	122,200	34.7	67.5
Community Industry	3,500	5.9	9.1
Youth Employment Subsidy	32,000	} 2.7	} 5.4
Recruitment Subsidy for school leavers (now YES)	30,100		
Job Introduction Scheme for disabled people	145	—	0.1
Work Experience Programme	44,300	0.6	14.4
Small Firms Employment Subsidy	3,600	—	2.0
TOTAL	628,645	137.9	315.0

	Total no who have benefited	Cost 1976/77 £m	Cost 1977/78 £m
Special training courses for young people run by MSC	3,400	11.9	17.6
Special measures to maintain training opportunities with employers for young people	29,300	22.0	37.7
TOTAL	32,700	33.9	55.3

References

1 The viewpoint that organizations can best be understood in relation to their environment has become influential in organization theory. See, for example, the 'contingency' approach of Lawrence P R and Lorsch J W, *Organization and Environment, Managing Differentiation and Integration*, Harvard University Press, 1967, or the 'open socio-technical systems' approach recently outlined in Warmington Allan et al, *Organizational Behaviour and Performance, An Open Systems Approach to Change*, Macmillan, 1977.

2 MORRELL James, 25 years back: The pace of change in *2002 Britain Plus 25*, Henley Centre for Forecasting, 1977 pp 7–11. The data quoted refers to changes in the period 1952–1977

3 NIVEN Mary M, *Personnel Management 1913–1963*, IPM, 1978, p 114

4 FLANDERS A, *Management and Unions*, Faber and Faber, 1970, pp 111–112

5 DONOVAN Lord, Chairman, *Royal Commission on Trade Unions and Employers Associations* Report, HMSO, 1968

6 NATIONAL BOARD FOR PRICES AND INCOMES, *Payments by Results*, Report No 65, Cmnd 3627, 1967, p 76

7 NATIONAL BOARD FOR PRICES AND INCOMES, op cit, p 10

8 The ability of work groups to manipulate bonus schemes has received considerable attention in the literature. Relevant studies include Roethlisberger F L and Dickson W J, *Management and the Worker*, Harvard University Press, 1939; Mayo G E, *The Human Problems of an Industrial Civilization*, Harvard University Press, 1940; Lupton

Tom, *On the Shop Floor*, Pergamon, 1963; Brown William *Piecework Bargaining*, Heinemann, 1973

9   WEBB S and B, *Industrial Democracy*, Longman Green, 1897, Chapters X and XI

10   ROYAL COMMISSION ON TRADE UNIONS AND EMPLOYER'S ASSOCIATIONS SECRETARIAT, *Productivity Bargaining and Restricted Labour Practices*, Research Paper No 4, HMSO, 1967, p 49

11   BLACKABY F T (ed), *British Economic Policy 1960–1974*, Cambridge University Press, 1978

12   NATIONAL ECONOMIC DEVELOPMENT COUNCIL, *Conditions Favourable to Faster Growth*, HMSO, 1963

13   Quoted in Clegg H A, *The System of Industrial Relations in Great Britain*, Blackwell, 1976, p 343

14   MORAN Michael, *The Politics of Industrial Relations*, Macmillan, 1977, p 18

15   PARKER S R et al, *Effects of the Redundancy Payments Act*, HMSO, 1974, p 4

16   The number of payments made under the Redundancy Payments Act are listed quarterly in the *Department of Employment Gazette*

17   Estimates quoted by Elliott R in Blackaby F T (ed), *British Economic Policy 1960–1974*, op cit

18   HUGHES James J, Training for what?, *Industrial Relations Journal*, Autumn 1978, pp 27–33

19   Ibid, p 27

20   DEPARTMENT OF EMPLOYMENT, *Training for the Future*, 1972

21   A large literature exists on incomes policies. Discussions of it are contained in Clegg H A, *The System of Industrial Relations in Great Britain*, Chapter 11, op cit; Hawkins K, *British Industrial Relations 1945–1975*, Barrie and Jenkins, 1975, Chapter 4. A history of the NBPI has been written by Fels A, *The British Prices and Incomes Board*, Cambridge University Press, 1972. A critique of the incomes policies of 1965–1969 has been written by Clegg H A, *How to Run an Incomes Policy and Why We Made Such a Mess of the Last One*, Heinemann, 1971

22   FLANDERS Allan, *The Fawley Productivity Agreements*, Faber, 1964

23   CLEGG H A, *How to Run an Incomes Policy*, op cit, p 66

24 PHILLIPS A W, The relation between unemployment and the rate of change of money wage rates in the United Kingdom, 1861–1957, *Economica*, November 1958. The views expressed in this article became influential among economists in the 1960s

25 ZWEIG F, *The Worker in the Affluent Society*, Heinemann, 1961, p 206

26 FLANDERS Allan, *Management and Unions*, op cit, p 8

27 MARSH A I and COKER E E, Shop steward organization in the engineering industry, *British Journal of Industrial Relations*, June 1963. The wider issue of the rise of shop stewards and their bargaining role has been analysed by Goodman J F B and Whittingham T G, *Shop Stewards in British Industry*, McGraw Hill, 1969

28 HAWKINS Kevin, *British Industrial Relations 1945–1975*, op cit, p 13. The topic of union growth has been dealt with in more detail by Bain G S, *The Growth of White-Collar Unionism*, Clarendon Press, 1970; Price R and Bain G S, Union growth revisited, *British Journal of Industrial Relations*, November 1976

29 MASLOW A H, *Motivation and Personality*, Harper and Row, 1954

30 HERZBERG F, MAUSNER B and SNYDERMAN G, *The Motivation to Work*, Wiley, 1959

31 McGREGOR D, *The Human Side of Enterprise*, McGraw Hill, 1960

32 MANPOWER SERVICES COMMISSION, *Review and Plan 1977*, p 9

33 Ibid, p 9

34 Statistics on long-term unemployment, *Department of Employment Gazette*, June 1978, pp 676–681

35 LEICESTER Colin, Recruitment in the '80s: reading the market and reducing the risks, *Personnel Management*, April 1978, p 28

36 PREST A R and COPPOCK D J, *The UK Economy: A Manual of Applied Economics*, Weidenfeld and Nicolson, 1976

37 JENKINS Peter, The map for Britain's journey into the Third World, *The Guardian*, 27 September 1978

38 JENKINS Peter, The industries that peaked a century too soon, *The Guardian*, 26 September 1978

39 HUDSON REPORT, *The UK in 1980*, Associated Business Programmes, 1974

40　RAY G F, UK productivity and employment in 1991, *Futures*, April 1978, pp 91–108

41　WRAGG Richard and ROBERTSON James, *Post-War Trends in Employment*, Department of Employment, 1978 or Britain's industrial performance since the war, *Department of Employment Gazette*, May 1978, pp 512–519

42　JENKINS Peter, The map for Britain's journey into the Third World, op cit

43　RAY G F op cit

44　BELL Daniel, *The Coming of Post-Industrial Society*, Heinemann, 1974 or Bell Daniel, Notes on the post-industrial society, in Douglas Jack D (ed), *The Technological Threat*, Prentice Hall, 1971

45　BELL Daniel, *The Coming of Post-Industrial Society*, op cit

46　The data has been taken from: Part-time women workers 1950–1972, *Department of Employment Gazette*, November 1973, p 1089, and *Department of Employment British Labour Statistics Year Book 1975*, HMSO, 1977, p 34. Part-time working is defined as 30 hours per week or less. The figures for manufacturing industry form a continuous series but the figures for industry as a whole are drawn from various surveys and should be treated with caution.

47　Part-time women workers 1950–1972, *Department of Employment Gazette*, November 1973, p 1089

48　LEICESTER Colin, *Estimates of Part-Time Employment and the Normal Working Year During the Next 25 Years*, Institute for Manpower Studies, Mimeo Paper No IN 156, October 1977

49　TOFFLER Alvin, *Future Shock*, Bodley Head, 1970

50　For more details of industries and occupations involved, see Newton S C and Parker S R, Who are the temporary workers? *Department of Employment Gazette*, June 1977, p 591

51　MANPOWER SERVICES COMMISSION/TRAINING SERVICES AGENCY, *Training for Skills: A Programme for Action*, 1977

52　Quoted by the *Financial Times*, 7 December 1978

53　SCIBERRAS E, SWORDS-ISHERWOOD N and SENKER P, *Competition, Technical Change and Manpower in Electronic Capital Equipment: A Study of the UK Minicomputer Industry*, Science Policy Research Unit, Occasional Paper No 8, September 1978

54 McLean J M and Rush H J, *The Impact of Microelectronics in the UK: a Suggested Classification and Illustrative Case Studies*, Science Policy Research Unit, Occasional Paper No 7, June 1978, p 1

55 Wilkinson Max, Race for the $5 bn computer memory market, *Financial Times*, 30 June 1978

56 Quoted by Gamble P R, *How Computer Technology is Revolutionising Hotel Management Efficiency*, Department of Hotel, Catering and Tourism Management, University of Surrey, unpublished paper, 1978

57 McLean J M and Rush H J, op cit, p 6

58 Ibid, pp 4–6 and pp 29–35 and Wilkinson Max, Cars accelerating towards a computerized future, *Financial Times*, 27 October 1978

59 Daniel W W and Stilgoe Elizabeth, *The Impact of the Employment Protection Laws*, Policy Studies Institute, 1978

60 Greenwood John, Manpower policy and the European economies, in Torrington Derek, (ed), *Comparative Industrial Relations in Europe*, Associated Business Programmes, 1978

61 Rubenstein Michael, Dismissals and the law, in Torrington Derek, (ed), op cit, p 149

62 Collins R G, Age discrimination comes home to roost, *Personnel Management*, April 1975, pp 24–26

63 Jolly James et al, Age qualifications in job vacancies, *Department of Employment Gazette*, February 1978, pp 166–172

64 Bullock Lord, *Committee of Enquiry on Industrial Democracy*, Report, Cmnd 6706, HMSO, 1977

65 *Industrial Democracy*, Cmnd 7231, HMSO, 1978

66 Drucker P, *New Society*, 24 April 1969

67 Professor Stonier Tom, *Education and the Post-Industrial Society*, University of Bradford, unpublished, March 1978, p 5

68 From *Education Statistics for the UK 1975*, HMSO, 1977, p 17. The statutory minimum leaving age was fifteen years up to 1973 and sixteen years thereafter. For a comprehensive account of educational statistics, see Hutt R, Pearson R, Parsons D, (eds), *Education and Employment: Selected Statistics 1966–1977*, Hobsons, 1978

69 From Young people leaving school in England and Wales, *Department of Employment Gazette*, April 1977, pp 353–358

70 Projections for England and Wales referred to above suggest that the percentage of school leavers with three or more 'A' levels will increase to 11 per cent in 1990 from 8 per cent in 1975, those with 1 or 2 'A' levels to 9 per cent from 7 per cent and those with low grade passes or no passes will fall to 45 per cent from 50 per cent.

71 From DEPARTMENT OF EDUCATION AND SCIENCE/SCOTTISH EDUCATION DEPARTMENT, *Higher Education in the 1990s: A Discussion Document*, February 1978, p 2

72 From *Education Statistics for the UK 1975*, HMSO, 1977, p 21

73 The MSC estimates suggest that the cost could be in excess of £300 per man per month in the case of a man with two children and over £100 per month in the case of a 16 year old. Quoted in *Review and Plan 1977*, op cit, pp 86–89

74 EEC COMMISSION, *Worksharing*, unpublished paper, February 1978, p 2

75 LLOYD M, *Unemployment – Is Worksharing an Effective Weapon?* A paper to the IPM National Conference, Harrogate, 1978

76 LEVITAN S A and BELOUS R S, *Shorter Hours, Shorter Weeks*, John Hopkins UP, 1977, p 1

77 CLEGG H A, *The Implications of the Shorter Working Week for Management*, BIM, 1962

78 Quoted by LLOYD M, op cit

79 LEVITAN A and BELOUS R S, op cit, p 21

80 Some of these points are also raised in Evans Alastair, Measures to make the jobs go round, *Personnel Management*, January 1979, pp 32–35

81 TAYLOR Robert, Worksharing and worklessness, *New Society*, 23 November 1978, p 453

82 HUGHES John, Shiftwork and the shorter working week, *Personnel Management*, May 1977, pp 18–20

83 Measures to alleviate unemployment in the medium term: worksharing, *Department of Employment Gazette*, April 1978, pp 400–402

84 Quoted in CBI, *The Shorter Working Week: A Background Brief*, unpublished paper, July 1978

85 See CLEGG H A, *Implications of the Shorter Working Week for Management*, op cit; Leslie E, Overtime: the institution that will not die, *Personnel Management*, July 1977, pp 34–36

86   Measures to alleviate unemployment in the medium term: worksharing, *Department of Employment Gazette*, op cit

87   TAYLOR R, Worksharing and worklessness, *New Society*, op cit, p 454

88   Ibid, p 454

89   FLANDERS Allan, *The Fawley Productivity Agreements*, op cit, describes how productivity bargaining was instrumental in reducing overtime from 18 per cent of total hours worked to 7.5 per cent over a two year period

90   See Analysis of basic holiday entitlement for manual workers covered by national collective agreements and in wages council sectors, *British Labour Statistics 1975*, HMSO, 1977, p 113. The latest figures for 1977–1978 quoted in HMSO, *Time Rates of Wages and Hours of Work*, 1977, shows little recent change on the 1975 position

91   TORRINGTON D, Some comparative aspects of employee benefits in Europe, in Torrington D, (ed), *Comparative Industrial Relations in Europe*, op cit, p 103. The figures refer to April 1976

92   Measures to alleviate unemployment in the medium term: worksharing, *Department of Employment Gazette*, op cit, p 401

93   OLMSTED B, Jobsharing – a new way to work, *Personnel Journal*, February 1977, p 78

94   See INDUSTRIAL RELATIONS REVIEW AND REPORT, No 172, March 1978

95   Measures to alleviate unemployment in the medium term, *Department of Employment Gazette*, March 1978, pp 283–285

96   McGOLDRICK Anne and COOPER Cary, Early retirement: the appeal and the reality, *Personnel Management*, July 1978, pp 25–28, 41

97   SMITH Catherine M, *Retirement: The Organization and the Individual*, BIM, 1974

98   INCOMES DATA SERVICES, *Early Retirement*, Study No. 152, August 1977

99   Ibid, p 4

100   THE DEPARTMENT OF EDUCATION AND SCIENCE, DEPARTMENT OF EMPLOYMENT AND WELSH OFFICE EDUCATION DEPARTMENT, *16–18: Education and Training for 16–18 Year Olds: A Consultative Paper*, February 1979, p 1

101   EEC, *Worksharing*, op cit

102 Brief accounts of the policies of other European govern-
    ments are contained in: Special employment measures in
    EEC Member States, *Department of Employment Gazette*,
    February 1978, pp 163–165 and Measures to alleviate
    unemployment in the medium term, *Department of
    Employment Gazette*, op cit, p 285
103 TRADES UNION CONGRESS, *Annual Report for 1977*, TUC,
    1978, p 1
104 Ibid, p 588
105 Ibid, p 551
106 WALKER Charles R and GUEST Robert H, *The Man on the
    Assembly Line*, Harvard University Press, 1952
107 BLAUNER R, *Alienation and Freedom*, Chicago University
    Press, 1964
108 Ibid
109 TRIST E L et al, *Organizational Choice*, Tavistock, 1963
110 SAYLES L R, *The Behaviour of Industrial Work Groups*,
    Wiley 1958; Kuhn J W, *Bargaining in Grievance Settlement*,
    Columbia University Press, 1961
111 WOODWARD J, *Management and Technology*, HMSO, 1958;
    Woodward J, *Industrial Organization: Theory and Practice*,
    Oxford University Press, 1965
112 BURNS T and STALKER G M, *The Management of Innova-
    tion*, Tavistock, 1961
113 MCLEAN J M and RUSH H J, op cit; Freeman Christopher,
    Government Policies for Industrial Innovation, The ninth
    J D Bernal Lecture delivered at Birkbeck College, London,
    23 May 1978; Advisory Council on Advanced Research and
    Development, *The Application of Semi-Conductor Tech-
    nology*, HMSO, 1978; Department of Industry, *Micro-
    electronics: The New Technology*, 1978
114 MCLEAN J M and RUSH H J, op cit, p 20
115 HINES Colin, *The 'Chips' are Down*, Earth Resources
    Research, April 1978
116 Ibid
117 Both statements quoted in ELECTRONIC COMPONENTS
    SECTOR WORKING PARTY, *Progress Report 1979*, National
    Economic Development Office, January 1979, pp 6–7
118 SWORDS-ISHERWOOD N and SENKER P, *Technological and
    Organizational Change in Machine Shops*, Science Policy
    Research Unit, unpublished paper, May 1978

119 The problems of management and computer-controlled information systems are further discussed in Myers C A, (ed), *The Impact of Computers on Management*, MIT Press, 1967; Mumford E and Ward T B, *Computers: Planning for People*, Batsford, 1968; Rose Michael, *Computers, Managers and Society*, Penguin, 1969; Stewart Rosemary, *How Computers Affect Management*, Macmillan 1971

120 BURNS Tom and STALKER G M, op cit

121 Such organizational changes are further discussed by: Thomas John and Bennis Warren, (eds), *Management of Change and Conflict*, Penguin Modern Management, 1972; Frank H Eric, *Organization Structuring*, McGraw Hill, 1971

122 An interesting recent discussion which focuses on the role of the personnel manager within the line/staff analysis is contained in Watson Tony, *The Personnel Managers*, Routledge and Kegan Paul, 1977, pp 167–190

123 TOFFLER Alvin, op cit, p 101

124 STIEBER J, (ed), *Employment Problems of Automation and Advanced Technology*, Macmillan, 1966, p 375

125 WEBB S and B, op cit

126 MORTIMER J E, *Trade Unions and Technological Change*, Oxford University Press, 1971, p 5

127 JENKINS C and SHERMAN B, *Computers and the Unions*, Longman, 1977, p 83

128 A view expressed by T Webb, National Officer, Association of Scientific, Technical and Managerial Staffs, reported in *Financial Times*, 10 August 1978. Recent TUC policy is contained in *Employment and Technology*, TUC, 1979

129 op cit, p 47. See also Purcell John, Power from technology: computer staff and industrial relations, *Personnel Review*, Winter 1978, pp 31–39

130 WOODHALL Maureen, Investment in industrial training: an assessment of the effects of the Industrial Training Act on the volume and costs of training, *British Journal of Industrial Relations*, March 1974, p 81

131 Ibid, p 82

132 PARKER S R et al, *Effects of the Redundancy Payments Act*, op cit; Smith Catherine M, *Redundancy Policies: A Survey of Current Practice in 350 Companies*, BIM Management Survey No 20, 1974

133 BELL D J, *Planning Corporate Manpower*, Longman, 1974

134 See PARKER S R et al and SMITH Catherine M, op cit

135 DANIEL W W and STILGOE Elizabeth, *The Impact of the Employment Protection Laws*, op cit
136 INCOMES DATA SERVICES, *Redundancy Schemes*, Study No 175, August 1978 and Smith Catherine M, op cit
137 DANIEL W W and STILGOE Elizabeth, op cit
138 DANIEL W W, The high price of redundancy payment, *Personnel Management*, September 1976, pp 16–18, 35
139 See JONES Ken, *The Human Face of Change*, IPM, 1974
140 DANIEL W W and STILGOE Elizabeth, op cit
141 Ibid, pp 49–50
142 OECD, *Education and Working Life*, 1976, p 21
143 OECD, *Education and Working Life in Modern Society*, 1975, p 11
144 WHISTON Thomas G, *Education, Work and Leisure: Some Broad Policy Issues*, unpublished paper, Science Policy Research Unit, University of Sussex, September 1977, p 3
145 HAYES Chris, Groundwork for a flexible future, *Personnel Management*, March 1978, pp 27–29
146 BUTLER Rosemary, *Employment of the Highly Qualified*, Department of Employment, Unit for Manpower Studies, 1978
147 Ibid, p 27
148 OECD, *Education and Working Life in Modern Society*, op cit
149 INTERNATIONAL LABOUR ORGANIZATION, *Some Growing Employment Problems in Europe*, Report II, Manpower Aspects, ILO, 1973
150 OECD, *Entry of Young People into Working Life*, 1977, p 49
151 See DYMOND William R, Impact of wider educational opportunities on labour markets, life-long education, *Labour and Society*, Vol 2, No 3, July 1977, pp 311–319; OECD, *Recurrent Education: Trends and Issues*, 1975; Moberg Sven, Education, training and tomorrow's worker in OECD, *Work in a Changing Industrial Society*, 1974; OECD, *Recurrent Learning: A Strategy for Lifelong Learning*, 1975
152 INCOMES DATA SERVICES, *Special Leave*, Report No 155, October 1977, pp 5–8 contains further details
153 The general text which meets this purpose is Thomason George, *A Textbook of Personnel Management*, IPM, 1977
154 MUMFORD E, *Computers, Planning and Personnel Management*, IPM, 1969, p 11

155   On manpower planning, see Bell D J op cit and Bramham John, *Practical Manpower Planning*, IPM, 1978. The relationship of personnel and business planning is discussed by Allen K, Cannon J, Carby K and Johnston N, Personnel planning – the key to future business success, *Personnel Management*, October 1978, pp 50–53. Little has been written on the relationship of personnel and corporate planning as such, but in this context Ken Jones' account of rationalization and social responsibility in *The Human Face of Change*, op cit, is useful. The much neglected area of cost effective manpower decisions has recently been remedied by Cannon James, *Cost Effective Personnel Decisions*, IPM, 1979

156   The number of job changes in the economy as a whole have already fallen from nearly 11 million in 1973 to just over 7 million in 1976

157   HUNTER L C and ROBERTSON D J, *The Economics of Wages and Labour*, Macmillan, 1969, pp 390–391

158   ANDERMAN S, *Trade Unions and Technological Change*, Allen and Unwin, 1967, p 182

159   LUPTON Tom and GOWLER Dan, *Selecting a Wage Payment System*, Kogan Page, 1969 or Lupton Tom and Gowler Dan, Selecting a wage payment system, in Lupton Tom, (ed), *Payment Systems*, Penguin, 1972

160   STIEBER J, (ed), *Employment Problems of Automation and Advanced Technology*, op cit, p 473

161   For more detailed discussions on the planning and implementation of job redesign, see Birchall D, *Job Redesign*, Gower Press 1975; Carby Keith, *Job Redesign in Practice*, IPM, 1976; Hill P, *Towards a New Philosophy of Management*, Gower Press, 1971; Paul W J and Robertson K B, *Job Enrichment and Employee Motivation*, Gower Press, 1970

162   TAYLOR F W, *The Principles of Scientific Management*, Harper and Row, 1947

163   McGREGOR D, *The Human Side of Enterprise*, op cit

164   For a concise review of the topic see Butteriss M, *Job Enrichment and Employee Participation – a Study*, IPM, 1971. More detailed studies include Guest David and Fatchett Derek, *Worker Participation: Individual Control and Performance*, IPM 1974; Hebden John and Shaw Graham, *Pathways to Participation*, Associated Business

Programmes, 1977; Poole Michael, *Workers' Participation in Industry*, Routledge and Kegan Paul, 1978

165 GUERRIER Yvonne and MACMILLAN Keith, Developing managers in low growth organizations, *Personnel Management*, December 1978, p 37

Tables: sources of data

Table 1: *British Labour Statistics Historical Abstract 1886–1968,* HMSO, 1971; *British Labour Statistics Yearbook 1971,* HMSO, 1973; *British Labour Statistics Yearbook 1975,* HMSO, 1977; *Department of Employment Gazette,* various editions

Table 2: *British Labour Statistics Historical Abstract 1886–1968,* op cit; *British Labour Statistics Yearbook, 1975* op cit; *Department of Employment Gazette,* various editions

Table 3: The forecast of the London Business School (LBS), the *Economist* (Econ), and the Cambridge Economic Policy Group (CEPG) are quoted in *Review and Plan 1978, Manpower Services Commission,* 1978, p 9; the National Institute for Economic and Social Research (NIESR) in the *Financial Times,* 29 November 1978; Economic Models (Econ Mod) in the *Financial Times,* 1 August 1978; the Financial Times (FT) forecast in the *Financial Times,* 14 May 1978; the Institute for Manpower Studies (IMS) in Leicester Colin, Recruitment in the 80s: reading the market and reducing the risks, *Personnel Management,* April 1978, pp 28–31; the Cambridge Department of Applied Economics (DAE) in Hines C, op cit, p 1 and Warwick in Lindley R (ed), *Britain's Medium Term Employment Prospects,* University of Warwick Manpower Research Group, 1978

Table 4: PREST A R and COPPOCK D J, *The UK Economy: A Manual of Applied Economics,* Weidenfeld and Nicholson, 1976, p 51

Table 5: UNIT FOR MANPOWER STUDIES, *The Changing Structure of the Labour Force,* Department of Employment, 1976, p 5; New projections of future labour force, Department of Employment Gazette, June 1977, pp 587–592

Table 6: UNIT FOR MANPOWER STUDIES, op cit, p 6; New projections of future labour force, op cit, p 587

Table 7: New projections of future labour force, op cit, p 591

Table 8: UNIT FOR MANPOWER STUDIES, op cit, p 14

Table 9: Ibid, pp 18–19

Table 10: Ibid, pp 24–29 and Bain G S, op cit, p 12

Table 11: UNIT FOR MANPOWER STUDIES, op cit; The changing structure of the labour force, *Department of Employment Gazette*, October 1975, p 985

Table 12: *British Labour Statistics Yearbook 1975*, op cit, p 34; Part-time women workers 1950–1972, *Department of Employment Gazette*, November 1973, p 1089

Table 13: UNIT FOR MANPOWER STUDIES, op cit, p 8; New projections of future labour force, op cit, p 591

Table 14: *Training For Skills*, op cit, p 36. Reproduced by permission of the Manpower Services Commission.

Table 15: *Statistics of Education, Vol 2, 1976*, HMSO, 1977, p 38

Table 16: *Higher Education in the 1990s: A Discussion Document*, Department of Education and Science and Scottish Education Department, 1978, Appendix II, Table 5

Table 17: BUTLER R, *Employment of the Highly Qualified*, Department of Employment, 1978, p 12; Employment of the highly qualified 1971–1986, *Department of Employment Gazette*, May 1978, p 535

Table 18: BUTLER R, *Employment of the Highly Qualified*, op cit, p 7

Table 19: Ibid, p 7

Table 20 (Appendix): Department of Employment Gazette, February 1978, p 213

Bibliography

ADVISORY COUNCIL FOR ADVANCED RESEARCH AND DEVELOPMENT, *The Application of Semi-Conductor Technology*, HMSO, 1978
ALLEN K, CANNON J, CARBY K, and JOHNSTON N, Personnel planning – the key to future business success, *Personnel Management*, October 1978
ANDERMAN S, *Trade Unions and Technological Change*, Allen and Unwin, 1967
BAIN G S, *The Growth of White-Collar Unionism*, Clarendon Press, 1970
BAIN G S and PRICE R, Union growth revisited, *British Journal of Industrial Relations*, November 1976
BELL Daniel, *The Coming of Post-Industrial Society*, Heinemann, 1974
BELL Daniel, Notes on the post-industrial society, in Douglas Jack D, (ed), *The Technological Threat*, Prentice Hall, 1971
BELL D J, *Planning Corporate Manpower*, Longman, 1974
BIRCHALL D, *Job Redesign*, Gower Press, 1975
BLACKABY F T, (ed), *British Economic Policy 1960–1974*, Cambridge University Press, 1978
BLAUNER R, *Alienation and Freedom*, Chicago University Press, 1964
BRAMHAM John, *Practical Manpower Planning*, IPM, 1978
BROWN William, *Piecework Bargaining*, Heinemann, 1973
BULLOCK Lord, *Committee of Inquiry on Industrial Democracy*, Report, Cmnd 6706, HMSO, 1977
BURNS T and STALKER G M, *The Management of Innovation*, Tavistock, 1961
BUTLER Rosemary, *Employment of the Highly Qualified*, Department of Employment, Unit for Manpower Studies, 1978
BUTTERISS M, *Job Enrichment and Employee Participation – a Study*, IPM, 1971
CANNON James, *Cost Effective Personnel Decisions*, IPM, 1979
CARBY Keith, *Job Redesign in Practice*, IPM, 1976

CLEGG H A, *The Implications of the Shorter Working Week for Management*, BIM, 1962

CLEGG H A, *The System of Industrial Relations in Great Britain*, Blackwell, 1976

COLLINS R G, Age discrimination comes home to roost, *Personnel Management*, April 1975

CONFEDERATION OF BRITISH INDUSTRY, *The Shorter Working Week: A Background Brief*, unpublished paper, July 1978

DANIEL W W, The high price of redundancy payment, *Personnel Management*, September 1976

DANIEL W W and STILGOE Elizabeth, *The Impact of the Employment Protection Laws*, Policy Studies Institute, 1978

DONOVAN Lord, Chairman, *Royal Commission on Trade Unions and Employers Associations*, Report, HMSO, 1968

DOUGLAS Jack D, (ed), *The Technological Threat*, Prentice Hall, 1971

DYMOND William R, Impact of wider educational opportunities on labour markets, life-long education, *Labour and Society*, Vol 2, No 3, July 1977

DEPARTMENT OF EDUCATION AND SCIENCE/SCOTTISH EDUCATION DEPARTMENT, *Higher Education in the 1990s: A Discussion Document*, February 1978

DEPARTMENT OF EDUCATION AND SCIENCE, DEPARTMENT OF EMPLOYMENT AND WELSH OFFICE EDUCATION DEPARTMENT, *16–18: Education and Training for 16–18 Year Olds: A Consultative Paper*, February 1979

EEC COMMISSION, *Worksharing*, unpublished paper, February 1978

DEPARTMENT OF EMPLOYMENT, *Training for the Future*, 1972

ELECTRONIC COMPONENTS SECTOR WORKING PARTY, *Progress Report 1979*, National Economic Development Office, January 1979

EVANS Alastair, Measures to make the jobs go round, *Personnel Management*, January 1979

FELS A, *The British Prices and Incomes Board*, Cambridge University Press, 1972

FLANDERS Allan, *The Fawley Productivity Agreements*, Faber, 1964

FLANDERS A, *Management and Unions*, Faber and Faber, 1970

FRANK H Eric, *Organization Structuring*, McGraw Hill, 1971

FREEMAN Christopher, *Government Policies for Industrial Innovation*, Birkbeck College, 1978

GAMBLE P R, *How Computer Technology is Revolutionising Hotel Management Efficiency*, Department of Hotel, Catering and Tourism Management, University of Surrey, unpublished paper, 1978

GOODMAN J and WHITTINGHAM T G, *Shop Stewards in British Industry*, McGraw Hill, 1969

GREENWOOD John, Manpower policy and the European economies in Torrington Derek, (ed), *Comparative Industrial Relations in Europe*, Associated Business Programmes, 1978

GUERRIER Yvonne and MACMILLAN Keith, Developing managers in low growth organizations, *Personnel Management*, December 1978
GUEST David and FATCHETT Derek, *Worker Participation: Individual Control and Performance*, IPM, 1974
HAWKINS K, *British Industrial Relations 1945–1975*, Barrie and Jenkins, 1975
HAYES Chris, *Groundwork for a flexible future*, Personnel Management, March 1978
HEBDEN John and SHAW Graham, *Pathways to Participation*, Associated Business Programmes, 1977
HERZBERG F, MAUSNER B and SYNDERMAN G, *The Motivation to Work*, Wiley, 1959
HILL P, *Towards a New Philosophy of Management*, Gower Press, 1971
HINES Colin, *The 'Chips' are Down*, Earth Resources Research, April 1978
HUGHES James J, Training for what?, *Industrial Relations Journal*, Vol 9 No 3
HUGHES John, Shiftwork and the shorter working week, *Personnel Management*, May 1977
HUNTER L and ROBERTSON D J, *The Economics of Wages and Labour*, Macmillan, 1969
HUTT R, PEARSON R, PARSONS D (eds), *Education and Employment: Selected Statistics 1966–1977*, Hobsons, 1978
INCOMES DATA SERVICES, *Early Retirement*, Study No 152, August 1977
INCOMES DATA SERVICES, *Redundancy Schemes*, Study No 175, August 1978
DEPARTMENT OF INDUSTRY, *Microelectronics: The New Technology*, 1978
INTERNATIONAL LABOUR ORGANIZATION, *Some Growing Employment Problems in Europe*, Report II, Manpower Aspects, ILO, 1973
JENKINS C and SHERMAN B, *Computers and the Unions*, Longman, 1977
JOLLY James, Age qualifications in job vacancies, *Department of Employment Gazette*, February 1978
JONES Ken, *The Human Face of Change*, IPM, 1974
KUHN J W, *Bargaining in Grievance Settlement*, Columbia University Press, 1961
LAWRENCE P R and LORSH J W, *Organization and Environment, Managing Differentiation and Integration*, Harvard University Press, 1967
LEICESTER Colin, *Estimates of Part-time Employment and the Normal Working Year During the Next 25 Years*, Institute for Manpower Studies, mimeo paper No IN156, October 1977
LEICESTER Colin, Recruitment in the '80s: reading the market and reducing the risks, *Personnel Management*, April 1978
LEVITAN S A and BELOUS R S, *Shorter Hours, Shorter Weeks*, John

Hopkins UP, 1977

LLOYD M, *Unemployment – Is Worksharing an Effective Weapon?*
A paper to the IPM National Conference, Harrogate, 1978

LUPTON Tom, *On the Shop Floor*, Pergamon, 1963

LUPTON Tom, (ed), *Payment Systems*, Penguin, 1972

LUPTON Tom and GOWLER Dan, *Selecting a Wage Payment System*,
Kogan Page, 1969 or Lupton Tom and Gowler Dan, Selecting a wage
payment system, in Lupton Tom, (ed), *Payment Systems*, Penguin,
1972

MANPOWER SERVICES COMMISSION/TRAINING SERVICES AGENCY,
Training for Skills: A Programme for Action, 1977

MANPOWER SERVICES COMMISSION, *Review and Plan* 1977

MARSH A I and COKER E E, Shop steward organization in the engineering industry, *British Journal of Industrial Relations*, June 1963

MASLOW A H, *Motivation and Personality*, Harper and Row, 1954

MCGOLDRICK Anne and COOPER Cary, Early retirement: the appeal
and the reality, *Personnel Management*, March, 1978

MCGREGOR D, *The Human Side of Enterprise*, McGraw Hill, 1960

MCLEAN J M and RUSH H J, *The Impact of Microelectronics in the UK:
a Suggested Classification and Illustrative Case Studies*, Science Policy
Research Unit, Occasional Paper No 7, June 1978

MORAN Michael, *The Politics of Industrial Relations*, Macmillan, 1977

MORRELL James, 25 years back: The pace of change, in *2002 Britain
Plus 25*, Henley Centre for Forecasting, 1977

MORTIMER J E, *Trade Unions and Technological Change*, Oxford
University Press, 1971

MUMFORD E, *Computers, Planning and Personnel Management*, IPM,
1969

MUMFORD E and WARD T B, *Computers: Planning for People*,
Batsford, 1968

MYERS C A, (ed), *The Impact of Computers on Management*, MIT Press,
1967

NATIONAL BOARD FOR PRICES AND INCOMES, *Payments by Results*,
Report No 65, Cmnd 3627, 1967

NATIONAL ECONOMIC DEVELOPMENT COUNCIL, *Conditions Favourable
to Faster Growth*, HMSO, 1963

NEWTON S C and PARKER S R, Who are the temporary workers?
Department of Employment Gazette, June 1977

NIVEN Mary M. *Personnel Management 1913–1963*, IPM, 1978

ORGANIZATION FOR ECONOMIC COOPERATION AND DEVELOPMENT,
Work in a Changing Industrial Society, OECD, 1974

ORGANIZATION FOR ECONOMIC COOPERATION AND DEVELOPMENT,
Education and Working Life in Modern Society, OECD, 1975

ORGANIZATION FOR ECONOMIC COOPERATION AND DEVELOPMENT,
Recurrent Education: Trends And Issues, OECD, 1975

ORGANIZATION FOR ECONOMIC COOPERATION AND DEVELOPMENT, *Recurrent Learning: A Strategy for Lifelong Learning*, OECD, 1976

ORGANIZATION FOR ECONOMIC COOPERATION AND DEVELOPMENT, *Education and Working Life*, OECD, 1976

ORGANIZATION FOR ECONOMIC COOPERATION AND DEVELOPMENT, *Entry of Young People into Working Life*, OECD, 1977

PARKER S R, *Effects of the Redundancy Payments Act*, HMSO, 1974

PAUL W J and ROBERTSON K B, *Job Enrichment and Employee Motivation*, Gower Press, 1970

PHILLIPS A W, The relation between unemployment and the rate of change of money wage rates in the United Kingdom, 1861–1957, *Economica*, November 1958

POOLE Michael, *Workers' Participation in Industry*, Routledge and Kegan Paul, 1978

RAY G F, UK productivity and employment in 1991, *Futures*, April, 1978, pp 91–108

ROETHLISBERGER F L and DICKSON W J, *Management and the Worker*, Harvard University Press, 1939

ROSE Michael, *Computers, Managers and Society*, Penguin, 1969

RUBENSTEIN Michael, Dismissals and the law, in Torrington Derek, (ed), below

SAYLES L R, *The Behaviour of Industrial Work Groups*, Wiley, 1958

SCIBERRAS E, SWORDS-ISHERWOOD N and SENKER P, *Competition, Technical Change and Manpower in Electronic Capital Equipment: A Study of the UK Minicomputer Industry*, Science Policy Research Unit, Occasional Paper No 8, September 1978

SMITH Catherine M, *Retirement: The Organization and the Individual*, BIM, 1974

STIEBER J, (ed), *Employment Problems of Automation and Advanced Technology*, Macmillan, 1966

STEWART Rosemary, *How Computers Affect Management*, Macmillan, 1971

PROFESSOR STONIER Tom, *Education and the Post-Industrial Society*, University of Bradford, unpublished, March 1978

SWORDS-ISHERWOOD N and SENKER P, *Technological and Organization Change in Machine Shops*, Science Policy Research Unit, unpublished paper, May 1978

TAYLOR F W, *The Principles of Scientific Management*, Harper and Row, 1947

TAYLOR Robert, Worksharing and worklessness, *New Society*, 23 November 1978

THOMAS John and BENNIS Warren, (eds), *Management of Change and Conflict*, Penguin Modern Management, 1972

THOMASON George, *A Textbook of Personnel Management*, IPM, 1978

TOFFLER Alvin, *Future Shock*, Bodley Head, 1970

TORRINGTON Derek, (ed), *Comparative Industrial Relations in Europe,* Associated Business Programmes, 1978

TORRINGTON D, Some comparative aspects of employee benefits, in Europe, in Torrington D, (ed), *Comparative Industrial Relations in Europe,* April 1976

TRADES UNION CONGRESS, *Annual Report for 1977,* TUC, 1978

TRADES UNION CONGRESS, *Employment and Technology,* TUC, 1979

TRIST E L et al, *Organizational Choice,* Tavistock, 1963

WALKER Charles R and GUEST Robert H, *The Man on the Assembly Line,* Harvard University Press, 1952

WARMINGTON Allan, *Organizational Behaviour and Performance, An Open Systems Approach to Change,* Macmillan, 1977

WATSON Tony, *The Personnel Managers,* Routledge and Kegan Paul, 1977

WEBB S and B, *Industrial Democracy,* Longman Green, 1897

WHISTON Thomas G, *Education, Work and Leisure: Some Broad Policy Issues,* unpublished paper, Science Policy Research Unit, University of Sussex, September 1977

WILKINSON Max, Cars accelerating towards a computerized future, *Financial Times,* 27 October 1978

WILKINSON Max, Race for the $5 bn computer memory market, *Financial Times,* 30 June 1978

WOODHALL Maureen, Investment in industrial training: an assessment of the effects of the Industrial Training Act on the volume and costs of training, *British Journal of Industrial Relations,* March 1974

WOODWARD J, *Management and Technology,* HMSO, 1958

WOODWARD J, *Industrial Organization: Theory and Practice,* Oxford University Press, 1965

WRAGG Richard and ROBERTSON James, *Post-War Trends in Employment,* Department of Employment, 1978, or Britain's industrial performance since the war, *Department of Employment Gazette,* May 1978

ZWEIG F, *The Worker in the Affluent Society,* Heinemann, 1961

Index

Attitudes to work, 21, 89, 111, 134

Black labour market, 44

Careers, 2, 55, 98, 115, 121, 129-130, 134, 135, 136
Collective bargaining (*see* also productivity bargaining), 12, 13, 22, 51, 55, 56, 71, 84, 90, 98-99, 100, 104, 116, 121, 123, 131-133
Computers, 49, 91-94, 102
Contracts of Employment Act, 14, 15

Demographic trends, 2, 33-37, 44-45, 122
Discrimination, 19, 35, 54, 83, 107, 136
Dismissal, 19, 52, 53, 57, 69, 104, 106-107, 108, 124, 125

Economic growth, 1-3, 7-9, 30-33, 46, 52, 58, 82, 86, 110, 121, 122, 124, 125, 129, 134, 137
Education, 2-3, 21-23, 35, 46, 58-63, 64-65, 78, 85, 95, 98, 109-117, 124-125, 130, 131, 133, 136
extension of, 81-83, 87, 114-117

and working life, 58-59, 81-82, 83, 87, 109-117
Educational leave, 70, 101, 116
Employment Protection Act, 52, 124
Employment Subsidies, 52, 69, 85, 104, 124, 138-141
Equal Pay Act, 35

Full employment, 2, 8-10, 12, 19-22, 27, 51, 103-104, 121, 133

Graduates, 3, 61-63, 111-114, 124, 134

Holidays, 7, 53, 70, 75-77, 83-84, 100-101, 127
Hours of work, 7, 44, 46, 52, 70-73, 78, 83-87, 100-101, 127

Incomes policies, 16-17, 19, 104
Industrial democracy, *see* participation
Industrial Training Act, 16
Inflation, 1, 9, 11, 17-19, 51, 74-75, 85, 123

Job creation, 19, 20, 114
Job evaluation, 132-133
Job redesign, 23, 56, 89, 111, 130, 133-135, 136

Job Release Scheme, 79, 138, 141
Job Sharing, 70, 77-78, 87, 128

Labour costs, 73-78, 86-87, 94-95, 104-105, 126, 132, 137
Labour force, age of, 44-45
  by industry, 37-40, 122
  by occupation, 40-42, 122
  growth of, 2, 27, 33, 122, 125
  projections of future, 33-37
  skills of, 40-42, 122
  women in, 34-36, 43, 122
  young people in, 36-37, 122
Legislation, 1, 2, 13-14, 18-19, 51-57, 64, 83, 103-108, 123-125, 136

Manpower planning, 87, 96, 104, 126-129
Manpower Services Commission, 19, 28, 52, 81, 140
Microelectronics, 2, 48-49, 91-96, 100-102, 123
Microprocessors, see microelectronics
Motivation, 22-23, 89, 111, 115-116, 129, 134

Organization structure, 32, 90-91, 97
Overtime, 12, 70, 73-75, 83-85, 87, 105, 127

Part-time working, 35, 43, 70, 77, 79, 83, 127
Participation, 55-57, 97, 116, 124, 130, 135-136
Pay and payment systems, 10-12, 55, 71, 75, 100, 125, 127, 132-133
Personnel planning, see manpower planning
Productivity, 9, 13, 17-18, 30-33, 46, 51, 71, 74, 78, 87, 90, 94-95, 98, 101, 104, 121, 125, 127

Productivity bargaining, 16-18, 87, 100-101, 104

Recruitment, 10, 54, 77, 101, 105, 127-128, 130-133
Redundancy, 2, 15-16, 19-20, 51-52, 54, 69, 98, 100, 103-107, 121, 124-125, 129-130, 132
Retirement, 37, 77-78, 83, 85, 105
  early, 53, 70, 78-81, 83-87, 101, 105, 127-128, 132

Sabbatical leave, see educational leave
School leavers, 3, 59-61, 109, 111, 114, 124, 134
Selection, 54, 108, 130-131
Sex Discrimination Act, 35
Shiftwork, 70, 72, 75, 83-84, 87, 127
Silicon chip, see microelectronics
Skills, 2, 12, 40-41, 47-48, 50-51, 73, 79, 96, 100, 109, 111, 114-115, 122, 127-128, 130-131, 133
Social change, 2, 21-23, 51, 56, 81, 116, 121-123, 125, 130, 136

Technical change, 2, 15, 30, 33, 38-41, 46-50, 58, 64, 71, 81, 88-102, 115-116, 122-123, 125, 128-137
  managers and, 96-98
  trade unions and, 98-102
Temporary work, 44, 83, 105, 127, 132
Trade unions, 2, 9-11, 15, 17, 22, 55, 71-75, 78-79, 81, 84-86, 90, 98-102, 104-105, 110, 121, 127, 131-132, 137
Training, 51, 81-85, 87, 95-96, 98, 100-101, 103, 105-107, 111, 114-117, 124, 129, 132, 136-137, 140-141

Unemployment, 2, 8-10, 16, 18-20, 22, 27-33, 46, 50, 52, 57, 64, 69-87, 95, 100, 104-107, 110-111, 121-125, 133, 137-138
forecasts of, 30-31
and young people, 28, 69, 82-83, 85

Wages and wage payment systems, *see* pay and payment systems
Word processors, 93
Worksharing, 52, 69-87, 101, 121, 127-128
the EEC and, 70, 82-84, 86
organizations and, 86-87
trade unions and, 84-86

New from IPM

COST EFFECTIVE PERSONNEL DECISIONS

James Cannon

The purpose of this book is to introduce a subject that is of relevance to personnel and line management alike and one that is of growing importance as the costs of employing people continue to rise. The author is not attempting here to push forward the frontiers of cost-benefit analysis, but rather to explore some of the simple decisions that are continually being made in personnel management, and to see how from an understanding of the costs and benefits of different decisions these might be made with a better knowledge of the consequences of those decisions.

Beginning with an introductory overview with examples of some of the more common decisions and how a cost benefit approach might help, the book goes on to examine a strategic selection of the issues and problems that personnel executives and line managers face every day. Focussing first on absence and how a cost-benefit approach might help in efforts to control it, the author then considers the problem of recruitment and labour turnover. Chapters follow on the cost-benefit equations of education and training, on research into management style, on the problems of payment systems and on human resource accounting. The author then examines ways of implementing cost effective decision making, plans and programmes before looking to the future to assess the threats and opportunities of the silicon chip for people in organizations.

1979   0 85292 253 1   hardback